LIVING LIKE A CHRYSALIS

LIVING LIKE A CHRYSALIS

JOHN COLBOURN

GLORY TO GLORY PUBLICATIONS

First published in Great Britain in 2014 by
Glory to Glory Publications, an imprint of Buy Research Ltd.
Glory to Glory Publications
PO Box 212 SAFFRON WALDEN CB10 2UU

www.glorytoglory.co.uk

ISBN 978 0 9926674 1 2

Printed in Great Britain by Imprint Digital, Exeter

Contents

INTRODUCTION 'FROM THE CHRYSALIS'   7

1. GRASPING THE MEANING   13
2. BEGINNINGS   21
3. A SOLITARY STORY   31
4. JESUS' BAPTISM   37
5. THE MESSAGE   45
6. CASTING OUT DEMONS   55
7. THE TRANSFIGURATION   65
8. THE FINAL WEEK   75
9. THE LAST SUPPER   85
10. COMPLETING HIS TASK   97
11. THE CROSS   107
12. RESURRECTION   119
13. PERSPECTIVES   131

SUGGESTIONS FOR DISCUSSION   137

I ask the reader to compare everything I say or write with what is written in the Bible and, if at any point a conflict is found, always to rely upon the clear teaching of scripture.

INTRODUCTION
'From the Chrysalis'
See 1 Corinthians 13:12 and James 4:14b

Do you sometimes stop in sheer wonderment when you look at the natural world? Can we ever stop marvelling at what is all around us, even the way our own bodies work? It seems that science never stops finding out more about things with which our human race has lived for thousands of years yet has not understood before the modern period. There are the great distances, so vast that we cannot comprehend them, such as the billions of light years spoken of by astronomers, and all the wonders of outer space. At the same time there is medical science which, in the lifetime of many of us, has given us what flows from understanding something of the marvellous structure of our DNA.

Things change in the natural world of course – we only have to see how propagation leads to new plant varieties. How can anyone imagine that there is no mind behind the wonders around us, that nothing was planned? When new scientific *discoveries* are made, we see them as that – discoveries of what is there, not creation by mankind. And we are not just led to applaud those whose skill has made each discovery, but we also wonder at and appreciate what has been revealed.

There are many other facts which have been seen and known all along yet which can seem to us just as amazing. One of these, surely, must be the way in which a caterpillar becomes a butterfly. In the early stage there is a small caterpillar, crawling along on the ground or climbing up on to plants, spending so much of its time munching leaves – to the dismay of gardeners who find their prize plants decimated! A caterpillar is small, though may grow to be larger compared with others; it is confined because of its nature to a very restricted area near the place where it started its life, usually a matter of a few yards.

But all the time it is awaiting a change into something so very different, for ahead of it is the destiny of being a beautiful butterfly. As such it will be free to fulfil its life purpose (which is the reproduction process of laying the eggs of the next generation). It is going to be free from restrictions, able to fly as well as move on the ground, set free from the immediate confines of a limited location. Butterflies have been proved to be able even to cross oceans.

So how does the change come about? By going through the chrysalis stage. When the time comes (and well we may ask how it knows when that is) the crawling caterpillar takes itself into an in-between stage. That means getting into a suitable place, perhaps on the stem of a plant, and transforming itself into something that is confined, unable to move about at all, to feed or seemingly do anything. It is accepting restrictions from the comparative freedom of moving about which it has been enjoying since it first hatched out. It is tied by the nature of being a chrysalis to almost total constraint. But all the time it is being prepared for that great day. Then when the time comes, it is able to burst out of the chrysalis, spread out its wings, show all its beauty, and fly. Its destiny, the full life, has come, even if for the insect it is a very short life.

And how does the caterpillar know what lies ahead? No butterfly has ever gone back to being a caterpillar again! No chrysalis has gone back either. It is all, as we would say, 'nature'. But being a butterfly could not happen straight from the caterpillar stage. There has to be the intermediate step – the restrictions have to come before the freedom is experienced.

Has it ever occurred to you what a wonderful parable there is in all this for us? It is something that has been very much in my thought as I have moved from the more active stages of life to being older, but more especially very recently. I feel that I am in the 'chrysalis' stage in my life. Looking back, there have been the 'four-score years' of a happy and fulfilled life. They have been years of learning and of activity, busy years with many times of pleasure too; they have included forty years of parish ministry and then nearly another twenty years in so-called 'retirement', which many clergy know as a period of still being able to be needed and having a 'retirement ministry', a time without responsibilities but still being used in God's service to help in churches and to minister to people individually. Retirement has also been a time for growth in faith when more unhurried prayer has been possible, and through that prayer the supporting not just of family but the local church, the places where I have been helping, and especially the parishes where the 'active' years were spent. Who is to know whether through that prayer more has been accomplished for God's kingdom than in the years of much activity?

But now has come the realisation that I have moved into an intermediate stage. News was given to me that my life expectancy was likely to be short, perhaps only a matter of months. With that stage, as well as through age, the earthbound 'caterpillar' stage of my life seemed to be almost over.

It is in this period that I have been feeling, in a way unlike anything before, that God is preparing me for 'moving house', which is the way I like to speak of it. There has been a realisation that what I have been speaking about for so many years is soon going to happen to me. I feel that I have been given a glimpse – almost a vision – of a window ahead through which light is streaming, and towards which I am moving. The theory of eternal life is becoming more of a reality at the personal level, just as I have seen happen to many to whom I have ministered in their closing stages of life. Here is what we speak of as the 'blessed hope' of life in the presence of God. God does not need to prepare us for this until the time is coming closer, for there is so much that he wants us to centre upon for him here, and we are to take his word for it that he has a place prepared for us – even to having already 'seated' us there (Ephesians 2:6). That promise is what we needed, but now there comes the sense that there is so soon to come the breaking through from the restrictions of being older and less active, from the restraints of life on earth, even being 'in the chrysalis', to the wonder of God's presence, however much we are unable from this stage to understand what that life will be like.

But I have been finding something else too: as I look at the life of Christ, the wonders of what is contained in the four Gospels and in so much of Scripture, I am starting to see it all in a different light. There has been the tendency, as we all find, to want to look upon the events described in the Gospels very much from a human viewpoint. We are seeing how Jesus faced ordinary human life and we are seeking to follow his example in the way we order our own lives. We are trying to look upon Jesus as man, searching for the human Jesus.

But now I have been finding something quite different. It is seeing the Gospels, and in particular the passages describing what we might call the key events in the life of Jesus, not so much from the point of view of human beings, but from what God was seeking to achieve, to teach, to reveal in them concerning himself. It is all part of what we often call progressive revelation, the way in which stage by stage through the Old Testament, and reaching a climax in Jesus, God has progressively revealed more and more of his wonderful nature.

Sadly it is all too common to look on the biblical records of Jesus in a critical way, wondering whether they have been accurately recorded. But they are trustworthy, and we can confidently take the attitude that it is through these accounts that God has explained much more of himself. I have been increasingly amazed at the wonderful way that they fit together, giving a whole picture from which we are able to grasp more and more of the wonder both of himself and what he has done for us through Jesus – the message, the gospel ('good news') of our forgiveness and redemption.

So our purpose in the chapters that follow is to take this theme, to look at the Gospels if possible from a more 'heavenly' angle as we ask ourselves what God is saying through this or that particular occasion, and seeing how it all fits together (as does Scripture as a whole) to teach us what God has seen fit to reveal to us (for our religion is a revealed religion, not made up by man) concerning himself, the way to come to him and know him for ourselves, and the life for which we are destined when we reach that 'butterfly' stage and are set free into the 'glorious liberty of the children of God'.

I write from the chrysalis.

1

GRASPING THE MEANING
See Philippians 2:9–11

Have you ever wondered what a person who is a very familiar 'voice' on the radio is like to look at in reality? Unless you have seen a photograph of the person concerned you won't know, but we tend to form a sort of mental picture, perhaps with an idea about their age even though we have no evidence beyond the sort of voice that we hear. Then one day that 'voice' is no longer disembodied because you see the person concerned on television or in a photograph on the page of a magazine. The voice may be the same, but was the mental picture of the person anything like the reality?

Or it may be that you have to speak on the telephone to somebody in a business capacity. There is no reason for you to meet, and not many firms publish photographs of their staff! But you may even get to be quite friendly over the phone and feel that you have come to know each other. However on neither side is there any idea of what that person looks like. Tragically, that at times can be exploited for immoral purposes, seeking to deceive, such as through online 'grooming'.

Or again, you work out details of a journey, perhaps looking at the junctions you are going to watch out for on the map or diagrams on a satnav. Then when you make the journey and come to the actual place you find that, whilst the facts about the places were all perfectly correct, they look totally different – maybe not in the open country but in the approaches to a town, or there is a huge roundabout when you had envisaged a mini one. The same can apply when following signs through a town centre.

Whichever illustration we use, we find that what we have pictured in the 'mind's eye' and what is actually seen can be very different. It is not that the description is faulty, nor that the evidence it is based on is wrong, it is just that the mental image is far removed from reality.

There is something in all of this in the way that the Jews were looking, in the days of Jesus, for their coming Messiah, God's anointed one who was prophesied as coming to their nation. Because what they had envisaged was not in tune with the reality, they failed to recognise Jesus as being the long-expected Messiah, so rather than look at the facts on the basis of the prophecies that were being fulfilled, they looked instead at the mental pictures they had formed. They had picked up on the prophecies which fitted in with that which they wanted the Messiah to do, seeing the successor to David as being a warrior-king (even if somewhat different) who would lead the nation to freedom from the oppression of the Roman occupation, rather than the leadership of a very different kind (which we will see later) for a worldwide task of establishing God's kingdom, with Jews being just part of that.

It is interesting to note that the twelve disciples, even after they had been with Jesus for three years and had come to acknowledge that he was the Messiah, still were asking him when he was going to show himself as the type of king that the nation was expecting – holding that idea right up to the time of the resurrection (see Acts 1:6; but we note in passing that Jesus didn't say the disciples' question was wrong, and he didn't say he wasn't going to restore the kingdom to Israel, although he could not tell them when it would happen, so we too can look forward to fulfilment of the prophetic hope that he will return and rule in righteousness and justice on the earth).

Someone who maybe could not get the widely accepted ideas out of his vision of Jesus was the inspired forerunner John the Baptist. He had been the one who had said that Jesus was to be the Lamb of God who would take away the sin of the world. He had seen the Spirit descend upon Jesus at the time of his baptism. But still he either could not grasp what Jesus was really about or he was seeking confirmation. The result was that he sent messengers, some of his followers or disciples, to Jesus with his question.

The reply of Jesus was simple. He referred to the things that he was doing, which tied in with other prophecies. We can read the account in Matthew 11:1–6. It was his way of telling John to look at the right things.

But there is another message which we can find here. John was to be the greatest of the prophets, the final forerunner actually pointing to Jesus. But even to him was revealed by God only what he needed to be told. God expects us to look at the evidence, and here we think primarily of the scriptural evidence, rather than expecting everything to be revealed to us in some other supernatural way. We have all been given minds to think, and all the information that we need is there. It may not be all that we would like to know, but it is sufficient for us within the purposes of God.

Let us go back though to the time when John sent those messengers. Jesus quoted the passage from Isaiah 61:1–3. He used that same passage again in Luke 4:16–21 in the totally different context of the synagogue at Nazareth, when he was showing the nature of his ministry to the people amongst whom he had been brought up and worked as a carpenter – to those, therefore, who knew him so well as a man.

> "The Spirit of the Lord is on me,
> because he has anointed me to preach good news
> to the poor.
> He has sent me to proclaim freedom for the prisoners
> and recovery of sight for the blind,
> to release the oppressed,
> to proclaim the year of the Lord's favour."
>
> *Luke 4:18f, NIV*

It was all a question of looking at the evidence, and of seeing things in the way that God intends rather than holding on to our human ideas. And the things that applied in the New Testament days seem to apply today too. Mankind does not seem to learn! We accept that what God is seeking to do is the best, but it may not be quite as obviously such to us. Can we really try to see things in *his* way?

Right from childhood we have been taught stories about Jesus. Do you remember that old children's hymn by W.H. Parker?

> 'Tell me the stories of Jesus
> I love to hear ...'

It was a great favourite in years gone by but is seen as somewhat dated now as we tend not to have hymns with things for children to sing that are so obviously for them alone. However, when we look at it, that hymn seems to sum up so much of what has been not only the case in Sunday Schools, but right through into the approach used with adults. It has been to put the emphasis very strongly on the humanity of Jesus, the 'Man of Galilee', rather than on Jesus as the divine Son of God.

Perhaps the reasons behind this start with the thought that we want to think of him as the one who understands us so much because he lived as one of us. So we can bring our felt needs to him in prayer, knowing that he fully understands. What a comfort this thought has been to countless Christians down through the ages!

Of course there is nothing wrong in stressing the humanity of Jesus. A key part of our Christian faith is the wonder that God became fully man. It is a truth that is emphasised in the historic creeds of the church.

It is a truth that puts the emphasis on the caring nature of God and the wonderful depth of his love in that Jesus 'became man', a truth so wonderfully declared in Philippians.

> Who, being in very nature God,
> did not consider equality with God something
> to be grasped,
> but made himself nothing,
> taking the very nature of a servant,
> being made in human likeness.
> And being found in appearance as a man,
> He humbled himself....
>
> *Philippians 2:6–8a, NIV*

We will return to those words later on.

So very naturally much Christian teaching, with an emphasis on following Jesus and living as members of his kingdom, has centred on his humanity as showing us through his words and example how he wants us to live, speak, act, show love to others, and so much more.

Through the past century or more, with the increasing ability to look at the Gospel texts with more depth and see what lies behind them – through knowledge of what was happening at the time, not only with regard to the way of life but the political and other factors of the time – there has come to be a very great emphasis on seeking to grasp the questions of the historic Jesus and what he would have been like to meet, what people would have seen who met him.

Is there not a danger, however, of trying to reduce Jesus, by trying to bring him down to what we want him to be like? It is similar to going into one of those sweet shops where you can take a bag and 'pick and choose' how many of the large number of different sweets available you want to put into your bag – one or two of that one, more of another, rejecting others.

We can get back to something similar to that we were thinking about above, where the Jews had formed an idea of what they wanted, what they liked – and then expected to get that and not other things from their Messiah.

So ideas about Jesus that don't fit in with the currently popular trains of thought, or our felt needs, get rejected. Science and archaeology can be brought into it too, on the basis that what is understood and has been discovered now must be the ultimate truth and cannot be corrected – this despite the fact that so many of the things that were taught a couple of generations ago on just that basis have been shown to be incorrect because of more recent investigation. Some of the things that were discredited in the past are not treated that way now. Wonderful discoveries about the time of Jesus have been made and other things are still coming to light, confirming the truth of the Scripture.

Where is all this leading us? Could it be that we have to admit that all too often we have so stressed the humanity of Jesus that we have played down his divinity? He was (and is) fully human and divine. But what are we doing? Are we forgetting our own creeds? Put in very simple words, the understanding expressed in them is that the pre-existent Jesus became man. Paul speaks of Christ emptying himself (AV) to become a man. Perhaps there has been a tendency to take that too far, often with an aim of making Jesus easier for us to understand. Sometimes this has led to an approach that plays down the 'divine'. This can happen over such thoughts as whether because he was a man he still had knowledge that an ordinary person could know, whether about people or what was going on in the world around him.

The 'view from the chrysalis' is starting to put things in perspective for me. Instead of assuming that, as a human being, Jesus was as much 'in the dark' as other people would be in a situation, I began to try looking at it the other way. Here is the divine Son, living in a human body but still very much with his sonship, so why should we not give full scope to what that involves?

Our aim in all that follows in successive chapters is to pursue that basic thought, to assume that in Jesus we have the one who became man, initially here on earth for a short period in time – and what is time in the eternal viewpoint? He moved from the timelessness of eternity into this world to fulfil certain purposes that only such an amazing step could possibly achieve. (But we must not forget that he retains his manhood even in his present exalted state). Would it be irreverent to think about a member of the board of a company being asked to go abroad for a period to represent that company and forward its purposes? He was keeping in close touch even in days without mobile phones and email, by the use of prayer, for which at times he felt the need to get away. But of course no analogy can ever do justice to the full wonder of the biblical revelation.

Moreover, what Jesus was doing was far more than reacting to what was happening around him and seizing opportunities. Rather, we are going to try to see that at least in the major events of his life, and especially during his period of ministry about which we know most, Jesus was seeking through each of them to portray an aspect of the purpose of God for which he came. Put together, they present a whole that is so much greater than the sum of the 'parts'.

While we are going to restrict ourselves to some of the major aspects, it may perhaps help us to take similar thoughts on to the broader canvas and ask ourselves what he was seeking to portray, to teach, to reveal, and how he used the seemingly chance encounters not just to help the individual concerned but to fulfil that divine purpose.

All the way through, it is a case of not playing down the divine, but letting it come to the fore. There is no reason for us to deny to Jesus not just the knowledge, but also the spiritual strength – even when under extreme pressure – to be able to fulfil the plans of the Father. And to fulfil those plans at the level of what may seem to be to us (at least until we look more closely, perhaps in the light of the Old Testament's teaching about God) just insignificant aspects or details.

After all, we know that our Christian faith is a revealed religion – something that has not been made up by human thought and observation, but which God has shown to us, through which he has revealed himself. We speak of 'progressive revelation' as the way in which through the centuries of the Old Testament, and coming to a head through the ministry of Jesus, these truths about God were made known, often through building one idea on the foundation of what has gone before over time, until the complete revelation (as far as mankind is able to understand it) was made known through Jesus.

In our next chapter, we will look at how much of this works out in the record of the Incarnation of the Son of God.

2

BEGINNINGS

See 1 John 1:2–4

The points at which the Christian faith is most often attacked is where the thought of Jesus being divine really comes to the fore. That is particularly the case in the narratives of his birth and his resurrection. The claims we make regarding both run completely contrary to anything that is expected in ordinary life – for whoever heard of a birth where God was the father rather than a human male, or of somebody rising from the grave who was so very clearly seen to be dead?

So if we are to try to answer the questions that we have before us, seeking to see the life of Jesus from the angle of what God was doing, we need to make our starting point an examination of the Incarnation narratives as given in the Gospels of Matthew and Luke – two accounts that not only differ greatly but quite clearly come from different sources as well as being written for two different groups of people. In these chapters, we are going to tend to look more at Matthew than the other Gospels because it was written mostly for Jews and shows more than the others the way in which Jesus fits into the message of the history of the Jewish race, fulfilling their Scriptures. But for the purpose of looking at the Incarnation we will probably find Luke's account the most valuable.

If the accounts are accepted, it almost follows on that the divinity of Jesus is accepted with them. On the other hand, if these accounts are not accepted, they have to be explained away. And down through the years there have been countless people trying to do that, either because they want a reason for not believing or because they feel that their own intellectual presuppositions demand that they have to deny anything that surpasses the understanding of modern man.

They seek to deny revealed biblical truth by saying that such things are a way of writing down traditions that had grown out of greatly exaggerated memories which had been passed down through oral tradition, claiming that they suffered in accuracy because of that, so putting in many ideas that simply did not happen; or that ideas had grown up about Jesus that needed a particular doctrine, namely that he was God, and so the events were 'edited' to give a basis for that. Or such sceptics simply claim that it was all wishful thinking and was for an age where the 'story' mattered almost more than accuracy.

Such sceptical thinking represents a refusal by many people (including many scholars) to entertain what they find difficult to believe because of the particular anti-supernaturalist basis of our generation (found largely in the modern Western intellectual tradition).

To put it in another way, it is tends to be assumed that the logic of the human mind is greater than the workings of the Almighty God who has his ways and purposes. So what we are going to try to do here is something which for many people seems to have become unthinkable, a betrayal of the way of thinking they have been taught. It is to start with the premise that the biblical accounts of Jesus have been given us by God, and that through them he is revealing himself. It is seeing them as being more than just stories, or even the reaction of Jesus to what was happening around him, and rather seeing that these key points are crucial to our grasping the very message that God is wanting us, as a human race, to know and accept. Perhaps it could be said that if we limit what God can do to what we feel he should be doing, we are exalting the human mind as though it were greater or more important than the mind of God himself. And so often we arrogantly do just that, without realising what we are thinking, saying or doing.

So let us make a start at the birth narratives. Just imagine for a moment that we were looking in at the point when, before the world came to be, God was planning how his divine, eternally existent Son should enter the world. I don't want to appear irreverent in saying this, but I do want to imagine the weighing up of the options.

Of course, as a pre-incarnate person had appeared to Joshua as the captain of the Lord's host, seeming to be an ordinary man until he made clear that he was to be worshipped as God (see Joshua 5:14–15), so Jesus could just appear as a man in the midst of society. He could be a perfect man, the ideal of what manhood should be. But in that way he could not have experienced what it was to be fully man for he would not have experienced being born and childhood, let alone the wonders of conception.

Or there was the option of his being given the very best the world could offer by being born into wealth or respectability, into a family with power and influence. Such might be what we would expect to have happened. After all, he was to be 'born to be King', to be in the line, the family, of the greatest of Israel's kings, David, and prophesied to be born in David's home town of Bethlehem.

But would such a birth have fulfilled what was needed? He was not to be an ordinary king with the task of governing a nation (at least not in his first visit to earth, and his reign and rule at his second coming will be far from ordinary). As we will see more and more, this is where his purposes and the ideas of the first century Jews were so far apart.

23

Then there might have been the amazing event of God 'appearing', coming out of the Most Holy Place (Holy of holies) in the Jerusalem Temple. That would certainly have made sense to the Jewish people then, but we have already seen it would not have been 'taking our nature upon him'.

If those alternatives are (rightly) ruled out, we come to the central question that we want to ask in each of these chapters: what was God doing? What was he wanting to teach and to show through each particular event in the life of Jesus? Especially in that event of the Incarnation, a narrative full of wonder, much loved down through the centuries, enacted by millions of children every Christmas, yet so often treated as merely a story.

I well remember talking to the head teacher of a large county infants' school when they were planning their Christmas event. Each class was performing a play and most of them were based on traditional nursery rhymes or pantomime themes. One class was given the Nativity to present. I said to her that I was somewhat worried that the children in the school might easily get the impression of there being no difference in historical fact or importance between what was clearly a fairy story and the story of the Incarnation of the Son of God. Was this the impression we wanted to give? I still hold to that view, all the more strongly some thirty years on, as society has become more and more secular. Not just the children but their parents as well have been brought up in homes where the Bible is not regularly opened (if it is there at all). Children are not being given Bible teaching from those seeking to pass on their own faith. Of course what I said to that teacher did not change what the school did that Christmas or any afterwards! But perhaps there is food for thought.

What is God's message to the world in this, first for those living at the time, then for Christians down through the centuries, including ourselves? We have to see all aspects of the life of Jesus as being part of a whole, and that message ties up with the amazing plan of God for 'the redemption of the world through our Lord Jesus Christ' (as the Book of Common Prayer puts it in the General Thanksgiving). The tendency today seems to be to take each individual biblical account or story as a unit on its own. Perhaps that is rather like what we are prone to do with our bodies – we look at a medical problem in one part as though it was not related to the general health and wellbeing of the whole person. The Christian seasons of the year, valuable as they are for ensuring that attention is placed in turn upon each vital aspect – Incarnation, the Life of Christ, the Cross, the Resurrection, the Holy Spirit, God as Trinity – tend to encourage us to feel a few weeks after, say, Easter: 'that's the end of celebrating the Easter message for the next ten months' and to move on to something else. We are unhappy at the idea of singing a Christmas carol in the summer! But our gospel, 'good news', stands as a whole that is complete.

We need to see that the biblical account of the Incarnation is essential to our understanding of God. Then we can start to see why in Jesus' self-revelation (and thus his revelation of who God is) these particular narratives are crucial. These accounts show us that it is all part of the divine purpose, that Jesus is the incarnate only-begotten eternal Son of God, true God and true man, that the Son is also the pre-existent Word, and that the Spirit was at work in the virginal conception of Jesus and at every other stage. The significance of the passion, death and resurrection can only be understood if we know who Jesus is, and the birth narratives (including John 1) show us his true identity.

Our belief is that God became man in Jesus. And God does not do things by halves! So Jesus was (and is) both *fully* God and *fully* man. He was not half God and half man.

He was not God only for the last few years of his earthly life.

Some have put forward the idea that the divine entered Jesus when the Spirit came upon him at his baptism (more about that later) but that would have meant that he was only divine for the last tenth of his life – could that have been spoken about as knowing what human life is really about and sharing our humanity so that eternally he is able to intercede for us in the way described in Hebrews?

Our belief is also that what Jesus did was not just for the Jews but for the whole world, so we need to look in these Incarnation narratives to see how that aspect is being worked out too. The answer must surely lie in part in the message of Simeon, based on the Old Testament, that Jesus was a 'Light to lighten the Gentiles' as well as being the glory of Israel.

So how did God organise the publicity for this world-changing event? What were the equivalent of press releases coming from 'on high'? If Jesus has just been born in the Bethlehem stable without the explanation and without people being made aware of what it meant, the people who were to witness it and all those through the centuries who have had to see that message not through their own interpretation but with the message that God wanted to bring through it, they could easily have lost that central message.

We may be full of wonder at the birth narratives that are speaking of things happening which are outside our ordinary scientific understanding or imagination. But with something so unprecedented and historically unique we can hardly be surprised at that! We are too prone to forget that God is God. We are tempted to think that our own understanding is the climax of all understanding, and are often too proud to acknowledge that God's mind is far greater than our minds.

"For my thoughts are not your thoughts,
neither are your ways my ways,"
declares the LORD.
"As the heavens are higher than the earth,
so are my ways higher than your ways
and my thoughts than your thoughts"

Isaiah 55:8–9, NIV

A salutary message indeed. So how did God work out the publicity for perhaps the greatest event in history – 'his-story'? The plan was for the birth of the forerunner, John the Baptist; then the coming of Jesus; followed by making him known (the idea behind 'epiphany'). First, there had to be the birth of John. One thing that is not easy to understand is how both Zechariah and Elizabeth were both clearly descendants of Aaron and thus of the tribe of Levi, while the two genealogical tables show both Mary and Joseph as descended from David, who was of the tribe of Judah; we have to accept that there are things we would like to know but which are not made clear to us, for God has revealed what we need to be able to understand. But the indication from this for us may be that Jesus was from not just an obscure Galilean family but had 'connections', if I can put it that way, with those in the Temple. Might this be part of the answer to the question as to why he was welcomed among the teachers in the Temple when twelve years old?

The announcement to Zechariah took place when he was performing, perhaps for the only time in his life, the task of offering incense at the altar right in front of the curtain or veil of the Temple. It was the most appropriate place, just feet from where God was perceived to be dwelling with his people. The subsequent narrative shows the impact that the birth of John had upon the people of Judea.

Then we have the way in which the greatest announcement was made first to Mary and then to Joseph. The same messenger, Gabriel, who had met Zechariah in the Temple went to the humble home of Mary in the despised (at least by the Jerusalem elite) Galilee. Such differences don't matter with God! The message was what counted. For Mary, a personal visitor was clearly the best way; for Joseph the message came through a vision. Perhaps in these modern days, when we want evidence all the way, it is harder to accept that our God may choose to reveal himself in a dream or vision. It is hard for us to grasp the impact the situation would have had on Joseph. We are quite used to couples who are not married living together, but how different then. To be 'betrothed' or engaged meant to be treated in terms of commitment as being in a permanent married relationship – hence 'your wife', and any breach of the relationship, even though not living together in marriage, was seen as adultery with dire consequences. God was asking a lot of Joseph, but that was the way he chose in order to bring about the birth of Jesus into an ordinary, stable home with both 'parents' absolutely committed to giving him an ordinary upbringing.

Who but God would have worked out such a plan? How else could the overall scheme be fulfilled, if it was not at great cost to a few key people?

It was one thing for the baby to be born, but how would God's publicity machine make sure that this event, affecting a couple in a very difficult situation and in a crowded town during a special event, 'make the headlines'? For us, it might perhaps attract a one-minute slot on the regional television news, or be totally ignored.

So we have the lovely account of the shepherds, rather than a vision given to the local 'clergy' or community leaders. Shepherds then had one of the toughest, roughest jobs, and those who were shepherds were looked on accordingly.

How wonderful that Jesus was later to use their work for an amazing illustration of his own task. But here we have a group of these men, very ordinary folk, given the grandstand view of the time when 'heaven came down': the vision of the heavenly host, whose full-time job (if we can speak like that in relation to eternity) was praise in God's heavenly presence, were to give a concert to welcome the Incarnation of the Lord into the world, to mark the start of the fulfilling of God's plan. Just in case they missed the meaning, those few shepherds were first given an explanation. There is no mistaking the significance than God put upon that event! There is no other Bible narrative with which we can compare it.

So there we have it – four incidents in a short time-span, when messages were brought from heaven to Zechariah, Mary, Joseph and the shepherds, each incident vital in its own way. That is impossible to 'explain away'!

God had a message to proclaim: that Jesus was born to be the Son of God. That birth was to show that while he was to grow up fully man in his nature, needs, appearance and way of living, yet from the very beginning he had the divine nature.

I find myself asking whether we can from our position as members of a race that has failed and into which sin has entered (so that all have sinned and fallen short of God's plan for us and all other humans) we can even start to understand what it must have been like for Jesus. Surely he was aware, quite apart from the stories Mary would have told him, that there was no barrier between him and God the Father.

While making due allowance for his growing up, we remember that 'Jesus Christ came into the world to save sinners' – that purpose was there from the beginning.

Writing 'from the chrysalis' and seeking to see God at work fulfilling his purposes, there comes more and more the sense that this was part of the Father's overall plan, and that we need to look at it with our eyes fixed firmly on his plan, rather than just emphasising the aspects that we find easier to grasp because they are more in tune with how we feel our needs to be – such messages as the humility of Jesus, or self-giving, or our attitude towards strangers based on 'no room at the inn'.

3

A SOLITARY STORY
See Luke 2:46–50

As we are asking about what God was doing during the earthly life of Jesus, and attempting to see things from that slightly detached 'chrysalis' standpoint. We are trying to see why God put certain events into Jesus' life and why they are recorded – so we can hardly leave out the account of the boy Jesus in the Temple. It is the only mention we have of him during the thirty years or thereabouts between the coming of the Magi and the return from Egypt, until we come to his baptism in the River Jordan. If we don't accept that stories are in the Gospels by chance, we need to look at this one for deeper implications.

A sceptic might say that here was a case of a 'bright boy' whose mother had remembered an incident, then leave it at that. But we should look deeper. I do not believe that this was the first time since being a baby that Jesus had been to Jerusalem and the Temple, for the Jewish custom was to go up to the Passover if possible each year, at least as often as they could. But there was something different about this occasion, for the age of twelve would have been about the time for Jesus' *Bar Mitzvah* when he became a 'son of the law' as did all Jewish boys. In the eyes of the religious law, from that time on he was included among the men and thus had the rights and duties of a man.

It could be that the ceremony had taken place in Jerusalem,

and what better place for it. On the other hand it may have been at Nazareth in the local synagogue; my own feeling is that the latter was the more likely as there is no reference to it in the account we have here, and it was a very major occasion in every boy's life.

What it did mean is that he was now accepted as a man in the Temple and could attend the teaching sessions there, in what was almost a primitive university, as the teachers sat around the porches on each side of the Court of the Gentiles. In later years that was where Jesus went to teach. My belief is that such a place was the setting for the wonderful Last Discourse – John 15–16, before Jesus went to the Cross. But that is moving too far ahead.

We need to look next at the Jewish concept of the Temple, and in particular the Most Holy Place within it. We are used to cathedrals, and see them as special churches, large places for the major occasions and the place where the bishop has his 'seat', his *cathedra*. The Temple was totally different.

Right back to the Tabernacle in the wilderness, there was the thought of it being an illustration, almost a foretaste, of heaven – the various stages or 'courts' were all illustrating the route to approach God. First the altar for sacrifice for the forgiveness of sin, then the laver for the ceremonial washing, speaking of the need for purity before God; on into the building where we will just mention here the altar of incense, symbolising prayer, directly before the Veil that hid the place where God was thought of as dwelling in the midst of his people.

So the Temple was a place that spoke of God being present, a place that was indescribably holy. Jesus speaks of how oaths were sworn on the Temple. If the earth, the world, is spoken of elsewhere in Scripture as God's footstool, the Temple was the special place. It was almost as though, there, heaven (the real dwelling of God) and earth met.

Such is the background: Jesus is now recognised as a man and able to be in the Temple as such, rather than taken as a child and kept with the women; the Temple as the place of God's dwelling, perhaps one could almost say an outpost, a 'porch', of heaven.

Now we put the two together, linked to a new-found freedom for Jesus. His words are very clear; He had to be 'in my Father's house' (Luke 2:49). Every word counts here (as so often in Scripture). We don't know of other times when the Temple was spoken of in such a casual way as being God's 'house'; Jesus would not have learnt that from the rabbis who had taught him as a child.

So it was as though Jesus, knowing full well who he was and speaking from that basis with a mind that was able to grasp spiritual things in a way that astounded the teachers in the Temple, is bringing to a head the full knowledge of his person, and that the Father's home-in-the-world was of course his home as well, the place where he had a special right not just to be, but to feel 'at home'. It was as though he was saying to Mary and Joseph 'where else would you expect me to be?'

We come on therefore to ask why this account is there, as part of God's plan for the self-revelation of himself through Jesus.

Surely this is the clearest indication we could ever want to have that divinity did not come upon Jesus only at the start of his ministry but was already there. He was born of course to be totally human, but in him God became man (not the other way round); thus we find a reinforcement of the message we had earlier when we saw the celebration by the angelic choir of the divine becoming man.

It is, then, an indication that his understanding, even as a child, was not limited to what he was taught by human teachers. Later on, the question would be asked as to how 'this man' had such knowledge, since he came from an artisan family rather than those schooled in the Law.

The danger for us is that of trying so to stress the humanity of Jesus, as something that we find helpful and which we can grasp, that we fail to realise that while all that is true yet from the beginning there was no barrier between himself and the Father, and that thus he had access (if indeed that is a strong enough term) to the knowledge of heaven. In heaven he had (has) full divinity and so full knowledge, including a total understanding of the purposes of the Father. Can we really accept that for nine-tenths of his human life on earth that was withheld from him? He 'emptied himself' (Philippians 2:7, AV) but that was of the divine glory in order to be man. He took the humble position but did not cease to be the Son of God with a pure, sinless mind in tune with the Father.

So we come to ask why only Luke records this incident, and why this one only from those hidden years? Many feel that Luke, the companion of Paul, was able to meet the elderly Mary and talk to her during the long period that Paul was held imprisoned in Caesarea before being sent on to Rome, and that it was then that he gained his knowledge of the birth narratives as well as this incident. Perhaps it was because of the need for security, and owing to the opposition shown to the early church in Jerusalem that she had felt unable to speak openly; now the things she had 'hidden in her heart' needed to be spoken of before she died, and to talk to Luke, a Gentile, a strong believer and a man of ability who was writing the Gospel, gave her the opportunity that she had never had.

She may have shared many other stories – we can imagine them talking and talking! – but Luke had to make a selection. Books had to be handwritten, hand copied, so it was not so easy to write many down. How thankful we can be for his selection of this one.

It would be lovely to know more about those 'silent years'. Many fanciful tales were recorded in the various non-canonical books that call themselves 'gospels' but which were written in the early centuries and certainly not by eye-witnesses. We can ignore them. Jesus was living totally as man, to experience the regular work, the burdens, the joys and sorrows of human life. How? We know that Jesus lived an ordinary life as a craftsman, and 'carpenter' was a term wider than we would give it today, and we assume that Joseph died long before Jesus started his ministry. But these things which we would *like* to know are not things we *need* to know. God has given us, wonderfully passed down through nearly two thousand years, that which he knows will give his message, and with that we need to be content.

4

JESUS' BAPTISM
See Luke 3:21–22

We are trying to look, as though 'from the chrysalis' at the life of Jesus, to see why the Father, working through the Holy Spirit, has made sure that certain events are recorded in the Gospels, and now we come to one of the most prominent of these events. The baptism of Jesus in the Jordan marks the transition from the silent years into the final three (yes, only three, and some feel it was shorter than that) years, those of his public ministry. Here we find there is something very special in the form of the heavenly voice speaking of the Father's confirmation of who Jesus is.

First though we need to get a little of the background if we can. Modern research and archaeology in recent years has meant a considerable change of view. It used to be thought that whilst a form of baptism was used by the Jews to welcome non-Jews, Gentiles, as 'proselytes' into the Jewish faith, it was not used by Jews themselves. However, recently there have been found many ritual baths throughout the country, many in private homes but including a considerable number near the main entrance to the Temple. So it seems likely that it was common for the Jews (or at least the more 'religious' among them) in the time of Jesus to take a ritual bath before worship, where the idea of cleansing the body is seen as symbolic of spiritual purity ready for the worship of God. Such baths could be found in the more well-to-do homes, as well as the baths near the Temple. But neither would be able to cope if large numbers of pilgrims at the feasts (such as the Passover) wanted them, so it has been thought possible, if not likely, that the pools of Bethesda (north of the Temple area) and Siloam (which was in the old 'city of David' area to the south) were used for this, rather than as a water supply for the city.

All of this points to the fact that, in the minds of many people, to get ready for God would need a ritual bath for cleansing as part of the act of repentance. It somewhat changes the ideas we have about why the crowds who went to John sought a ritual cleansing action using the water that was available where they were – the river Jordan – to accompany their repentance. It would not have been a totally new concept.

Now let us turn our thoughts to John the Baptist himself. The last we had heard of him was just before the account of Jesus' birth.

And the child grew and became strong in spirit; and he lived in the desert until he appeared publicly to Israel.

Luke 1:80, NIV

Then there is silence until John suddenly bursts in on the scene, proclaiming the message by the Jordan, which was on the fringe of the desert area of the country. He was the forerunner, like a herald who would go before an important person telling people to 'make way' and to be ready to greet the king or other important person who would be passing that way. Linked to this is the thought that when a very important person was to journey down a road, and the roads were usually just rough tracks, the local population would turn out to do some road repairs in order to make the way smoother – hence preparing the way in the wilderness.

It would appear that John had not met Jesus before, although they were second cousins. They lived in different parts of the country, and with travelling being mostly on foot people did not visit friends and relatives at a distance in the way people think nothing of doing today. John seems to have been living 'in the desert'. We don't know at what point he went there, whether as a boy or when a young man. Nor do we know whether he was living on his own or in one of the religious communities (almost like monasteries) of the more devout men who were disenchanted with the religious life of the country at that time (such as the politicisation of much of the Temple worship) and chose to have a far more austere life. They included the sect of the Essenes as well as the community at Qumran, whose hidden library was found after the Second World War and came to be known as the Dead Sea Scrolls. There has been much speculation and scholarly study devoted to whether John had been in such a group, but for our purpose it is but conjecture and can detract from the scriptural emphasis upon John who saw himself as the one to prepare the way, the one who much 'decrease' as Jesus began his ministry, so that Jesus himself might 'increase'.

As to the content of his message (to which we shall return later) it was about being ready to be the people of God. We tend to think of the baptism as being the main part of John's task, but was it? The forerunner was there to proclaim. That proclamation brought a response within the hearts and minds of the people – which we speak of as 'repenting'. Repenting is a word for turning. To turn you have to turn *from*, in order to turn *to*. That needed some form of symbolic action, hence the use of the ritual washing or baptism. It was purely a washing to symbolise repentance, and not with the same meaning as Christian baptism. John led the people in that baptism.

Now we want to bring this together at the momentous day when Jesus came to the crowds by the Jordan. John has been forewarned, by the Spirit no doubt, that Jesus was on his way. In that, John knew the climax to his ministry had been reached, even though he would continue to proclaim the message and to baptise until after some unknown interval he was imprisoned by Herod – the account of which is outside our scope.

What we do want to look at are the questions (and in our 'chrysalis' way of trying to see why God is doing these things, and what he is trying to say to us by wanting these stories recorded) about *why* Jesus allowed himself to go through this ritual cleansing when he was without sin, and *what was the implication* of the hearing of the voice (of the Father) from heaven, not just by John but by those gathered round. As always when we come to the interpretation of Bible accounts, we need to put them into context, and that includes all that we can know about the customs of the time and the ways of thinking of those involved. That is a lesson I learnt many years ago through the (then) Palestine Exhibitions run by what was the Church Missions to Jews, throwing so much light upon the way of life in Bible, and especially New Testament, times. Those exhibitions did much to guide my Bible teaching ministry over sixty years.

John was preparing for people to meet the long-awaited Messiah; their expectation of the one who would be the Son of David was that he would be a political, even military leader who would save the nation from the power of Rome. That was the very big 'felt' need of the nation. But, as we will see in our next chapter, the kingdom Jesus came to inaugurate was very different.

Yet Jesus was coming to lead. He was not coming to

stand aside and tell people what to do. The message of the Incarnation meant that from the beginning he was to be man among men.

So in what happened we see all this being demonstrated.

Let us go back in thought for a moment: I underlined that repentance really means 'turning' as much to as from. With Jesus, however, there was no question of turning from any way of sin, nor of a way of any failing to give God the rightful place in his life, nor of sinning in thought, word or deed. He was sinless. But there was a need to come alongside those who were turning from sin to God. If he was to lead in the establishing of a spiritual kingdom, he needed to do it from amongst the people and stand with them in their commitment to a life of giving God his place in their lives. The entrance to the path of messiahship was to be the opposite to what was expected. He took the path of humility, answering John's question about whether it was not more appropriate for Jesus to baptise John by saying that John should allow it to be this way 'for now'. In other words, to use something of a military way of thinking, he was going to lead from the front, but at the same time from being very much one of them, one of the troops.

Thus we see the Father's plan for Jesus being *among* those he led. It was the path of humility, not of domination; it was a path that linked in with that which he had taken at Bethlehem. It was a path of identification as well as a shown commitment.

With that in mind we go to the other side of the account, the coming of the Holy Spirit – in a form that looked like a dove – upon Jesus as he came up out of the water (i.e. when the baptism, the identification, was over), and the coming too of the heavenly voice.

We want to stress that the descent of the Spirit in a visible form came after that act of identification and that it was in the identification that he embarked upon his public ministry. We can thus discount any idea that the coming of the Spirit was in any way becoming divine. It did not mean that only at this point did Jesus 'become' God as well as man.

Perhaps we can note something else that I don't believe is by chance: while we read of quite a number of occasions when the Spirit came upon people in the Old Testament, after the accounts of events surrounding Jesus' birth, and the ministry of John we don't have a great many references to the Spirit in the Gospels nor a great deal of teaching about him, until towards the end of the earthly ministry of Jesus. Could this be because of the need to stress that God is one? This is a vital article of Jewish belief with which we would totally agree. The doctrinal truth that Jesus was (all along) the second person of the Holy Trinity would be more clearly understood subsequently (though of course his divinity is already revealed and affirmed in the Gospels). The gift of the Holy Spirit (the third person of the Trinity-in-unity) could only be given to the Christians – the church – after the Ascension, when it was clear that Jesus had gone back to heaven.

Then we turn our thoughts to the heavenly voice, clearly that of the Father (the first person), which came at the same time as the baptism of Jesus. Clearly this was another affirmation of Jesus. He who had taken the step of identification was now going to be the leader from amongst mankind. The whole Trinity was involved, so God was showing forth that this was his plan. When Jesus was being baptised, those who at the same time had taken the step of turning to God – of renewing their allegiance – were to grasp that this was both the Lamb of God (see John 1:29), and the Son of God:

And a voice from heaven said, "This is my Son, whom I love; with him I am well pleased."

Matthew 3:17, NIV

Incidentally, this is not the only time when the Father's voice was heard. There was another occasion where affirmation was needed, and then the words were added that we are to *listen to him*.

So there we have it. We can see Jesus as man who stood in the midst of others who were (re-)committing their lives to God. We can see clearly his connection with the Holy Spirit, and Jesus is being totally affirmed by the Father as fulfilling his plan.

Now we have to look at the message that Jesus proclaimed, especially at the start of his ministry. And once again, it is not as obvious as it appears!

5

THE MESSAGE
See Matthew 5:3; 7:21

If you were to go around any congregation and ask the simple question 'What was the message Jesus preached?' you would probably be given a variety of answers. But predominant among them might well be that which we would also find in much of wider society (at least among those who know anything about Jesus), that above all he preached a message of love: the thought of God's love for us, and the need for us humans to show love towards each other. Hence we find that for many people the message of Christmas is thought of as being that of goodwill, and the season as a time to practise that, through giving both to family and to charity. It follows on from that in a logical way that Christians should be those always willing to help those who are down or in trouble, to be forgiving, to be at the forefront of charitable endeavour.

We are not going to dispute any of that; it lies at the bottom of the whole theme of a social gospel and the church reaching out into the world around. Perhaps more than ever such an approach is needed today. It is the way in which many people are going to be brought into contact with an expression of Christianity that seems relevant to their own lives.

But our question is whether this was indeed the primary message of Jesus. Was this his core message? Or are we centring on that with which we are comfortable? We need to go back and look carefully at what has been set down for us, all put there for a very real reason. When we do so we find a somewhat different set of priorities emerging. We need to see whether what we thought we found fits together as a whole message, both within one Gospel (here, particularly, Matthew), and between the four Gospel accounts.

Standing out comes the message that Jesus is spoken of as 'the Word'. It is a title full of deep meaning, but tied to the thought that, through what is said by a person, something of the identity and personality of the speaker comes out. So through Jesus, the 'living Word', we see so much more of the person, nature and character of God. In being he was (and is) the living Word, expressing the ways, the thoughts, the purposes and the message of God to us by what he said.

So having been thinking about how the events that led up to the start of the ministry of Jesus teach us much, we go on to think of the things that he said.

Matthew gives us the message of Jesus in a way that speaks especially to the Jewish people. God had chosen Abraham to be the special channel of his purposes two thousand years earlier. God's self-revelation was centred on the Hebrews, and it was through the Jews that the fulfilment of his purposes in the coming of Jesus would be brought about. They had understandings which others did not have. One of those was the concept of heaven as being a place of glory, praise and worship – even somewhere to aspire to, but which they did not as yet know how to reach. They had the record of Elijah being taken up into heaven, but the message they had been given was that their purpose in the world was to live out obedience to God's law as the best way to live. It was therefore to them that the concept of 'the kingdom of heaven' is used a great deal, as recorded in Matthew, but the other Gospels use the term 'the kingdom of God'. It was in Matthew too that we find the three amazing chapters we speak of as the Sermon on the Mount.

What was the Sermon on the Mount? At first sight it seems a single entity, a sermon preached on one occasion but perhaps it is something more. Writing as one who has preached a good number of sermons over a lifetime of ministry, I am well aware that preachers will use similar material in different occasions (and hopefully different locations!) with slight variations. They will come back to particular themes that they believe are very important, time and time again, and more especially when they have a ministry that takes them to different groups or congregations. While such a way certainly does not work in a single church, it can be the best thing when moving around. It is the normal way for evangelists. Retired clergy often help across an area, moving from one church to another when needed and can be known in the various churches because of a particular style of preaching.

Could there have been any repetition in the ministry of Jesus? Was the Sermon on the Mount typical of the sort of things that he spoke about? Perhaps the slight variations between this account and other times when we are told of his preaching are more to do with this than variations made between different people using 'sources'.

What, then, was the main purpose of his preaching? Let us start with one very obvious thing that it was not: it was not proclaiming a way of salvation, of forgiveness based on what Jesus came to do on the Cross. The Cross lay in the future, and so of course did the resurrection. Both are prominent in the preaching of the apostles and in the epistles. They form the major part of the 'core message' of the church; but they are not the aim of the preaching of Jesus. That is not to deny that they should be treated as of first importance in our preaching, it is simply saying that Jesus' preaching had a different aim.

Let us go back to the message of John the Baptist. We

are told in Matthew 3:2 that he preached "Repent, for the kingdom of heaven is near" (NIV). Then move forward a chapter, to 4:17 and we find that Jesus' theme was exactly the same words. He had come to bring the message of the kingdom of heaven to this world. He was the King, seeking to extend the kingdom. Then, later on, he was to speak of the kingdom, not as a future kingdom, but that it was 'in you' or 'among you' (translations vary). His starting to preach had brought a change as people were turning to him, so already the kingdom was being established as the members gathered around their King.

Probably then the best answer to give to our question is that the aim of Jesus was to set up a branch, a colony of heaven's kingdom – a phrase that would have meant much in those days when Rome was setting up cities as 'colonies' where the population included people who would not otherwise have had Roman citizenship but were granted it through birth in that city. Paul had Roman citizenship because he was born in one such, namely Tarsus. Jesus set up colonies of his heavenly kingdom first among the Jewish nation, and then that would later extend (starting not that long after the Ascension) to Gentiles.

So, as well as drawing people to himself and drawing them to respond to God's call through repentance, his teaching would establish the way of life which he expected – and expects – them to follow. Remember how in Matthew 6:33 he says: "Seek first his kingdom and his righteousness". The blessings of life with him would follow.

Then we find so many of his parables start with a phrase such as, "The kingdom of heaven is like..." giving an illustration of one aspect of what the kingdom is, as well as more direct teaching. In the Sermon on the Mount several times we have the phrase '... but I say unto you' as Jesus speaks with authority, his own authority, rather than quoting other teachers of previous generations. That was something the Jewish people noticed, for it was in complete contrast with the way their rabbis taught (and with the way of teaching still in the Orthodox Jewish community, where all teaching is based on developing the teaching and insights of those who expounded that passage or theme in the past, often centuries earlier; see Matthew 7:29 for the reaction to this type of teaching by Jewish people.)

As Jesus was preaching the message of the kingdom, we must move on to ask what the nature of the kingdom is. To grasp this is vital if we are to understand what he is expecting (and I use that word deliberately) of each of us.

A kingdom is that over which a king reigns, where he sets the laws. In ordinary terms, that must involve territory, and the means to enforce his laws. It should involve ruling for the good of those ruled if there is to be co-operation. But how does that apply over God's kingdom? After all, "God is Spirit" (John 4:24). Jesus said to Pilate, when acknowledging that he was a King: "My kingdom is not of this world" (John 18:36). In other words, it is a kingdom in the spiritual realm.

First and foremost, God reigns in heaven where he is totally acknowledged by the heavenly host of beings who are with minds and not in any way automatons. They delight to worship him, finding their purpose in doing that in a situation where time does not exist (time itself we see as part of the created order). They are there to do his bidding. The word 'angel' means 'messenger' and so the angels who sometimes come into contact with people, and whom we are told are watching over God's people, are some of those beings. We gather there are other 'orders' too, but we are not told as much as we might like to know!

Such then is the main 'kingdom of heaven'. But the wonder is that God has seen fit to want to set up what we can call 'colonies' of that kingdom here on earth, not just as we have seen in the days of Jesus, but we need to grasp that every Christian community, church, fellowship or whatever we choose to call it, is just such a colony. Let us get an illustration from something we know well – citizenship of whatever country we belong to. We live in an increasingly global society, so wherever you go in the world you will find numbers of other citizens of your own country – communities large or small, who are there because of work or just because they have chosen to live there. Of course they seek to fit in with the way of life and the laws of the country where they are living, to make friends with those who hold the citizenship of that country, to be valuable members of that community. But they never forget where their primary citizenship, and so their first loyalty, lies – in the country to which they belong. At the same time there are those who have come to the country and, while not forgetting their personal origins, have chosen to change their citizenship by being 'naturalised'. It was interesting to talk on a Remembrance Day to a group of primary school children, the majority of whom were descended from Pakistani families who had come to England a couple of generations ago, since World War II. The natural thought was that they would not feel that what happened here then was part of 'their' story, but the opposite proved to be the case, such was the extent to which embracing citizenship here had affected their families' ways of thought.

Jesus uses a parallel thought when he speaks in John 10 about his being the Good Shepherd, caring for his flock, then he goes on to speak of other sheep that he had who are not of that (the Jewish) flock, and how he must bring them in, bring them together, so that they will all be part of the one flock – which we would call the worldwide church of God.

All this can help us grasp our position. To be a Christian

certainly means accepting the message of the Cross and resurrection, whether through what many would speak of as a conversion experience or in a slow process of coming to accept and understand. But that *on its own* is certainly not what was the whole of God's purpose through Jesus. It is his plan that those people come together to form a community for living out the message, for showing how Christianity works and changes life for the good, for following the example of Jesus in service of the community and showing his love in action for other people.

Just as Jesus expected his followers to witness to their new faith through a baptism of repentance, so the way for us is through Christian baptism which still has the repenting theme, but adding to it a demonstration of what coming into the kingdom means through being united, symbolically, with Jesus' death and resurrection. Often it is accompanied with the sign of the Cross, our Christian symbol, being made on the forehead of the new member. Once I had the privilege of taking a baptism service in the Naval tradition on board a warship, where the ship's bell is turned upside-down to form a font. In the talk I asked if one of the officers had his cap with him. Then I showed how, on the cap, the badge was over the forehead, and symbolised loyalty both to the Crown and to the Navy. I then said that the cap and badge were put on and taken off, but Christians have the invisible badge of the Cross there all the time. Such needs to be our loyalty.

So the question arises as to how far we really share God's vision of the kingdom. Are we seeing the local church in the same way political parties have a club for like minded people in the locality? Is it almost our 'local' where we go to meet our friends? Or is it the centre of our vision to be a witnessing, out-reaching community, seeking to carry the message of the kingdom into the community all around? And from that it is but a short step to be asking whether what that community is seeing is a real reflection of God's kingdom, where his ways of love, mutual acceptance and reaching out to those around are evident.

An exercise that can be very useful is to list the parables of the kingdom, and then on your list write against each one the main aspect of teaching about the kingdom that Jesus is seeking to convey in that parable. Putting the picture together can help us see the root and purpose of his preaching message. To make it easier, look in Matthew 13, then chapters 20 to 22.

It is time to go back to our 'chrysalis' way of thinking once again. We are able from that standpoint to take a more detached view and see the wonder of what God is doing, looking at the whole rather than the particular situation that we find ourselves in with all the challenges of everyday living.

Has it ever occurred to you what an astounding thing it is that our wonderful God has chosen to use ordinary human people, whose life expectancy in our country is in the 70s but in many parts of the world and historically is far less, and to use such temporary residents upon planet Earth to build colonies of heaven's eternal kingdom, and that the plan of God in redemption has so far depended on perhaps eighty generations (the precise number is not relevant) and depends on them for the transmission of the eternal gospel message? The world has been here for thousands of years, yet he is using such a relatively short period to work out not just a way for people to live their very temporary lives, but to have access to the eternal kingdom of God.

It is not as though it was one plan amongst many. There is no other way of salvation. Jesus Christ came just once to set up the colonies of his kingdom on earth and teach us God's way.

Are we being faithful to him and sharing his vision, so

that his kingdom may continue to grow and God's people may continue to show forth not ways that *they* feel to be the best, but *his* way? To follow the way and teaching of Christ is indeed a challenge, but also a call to true dedication.

6

CASTING OUT DEMONS
See Matthew 4:10–11

Here is one group of the biblical accounts about Jesus which it is all too easy to dismiss with a sort of twenty-first century superiority. How could Jesus have been casting out 'unclean spirits' and demons? In our generation, many people don't believe that such things exist. They think it was just the way people without scientific knowledge spoke and that these were simply cases of mental illness. So they think that Jesus was going along with the way of thought of his time and they diminish his understanding.

Is that really the situation? The fact is that those who have had personal experience in this field, and have come face to face with situations when spirits have come to intrude into a person's life even if not to the extent of 'demon possession', are left in no doubt about the reality of what has happened. Such things are happening today, and not just in 'Third World' situations. They have happened down through the centuries and they happened in the days of Jesus. We could go farther and say that there was a reason for them happening particularly during the time of Jesus, and a reason for them happening in somewhat different forms today. So taking our 'chrysalis view' of an understanding of the events and purposes in the life of Jesus, this is the second and last of the more general subjects (as against specific incidents) to which we need to turn our attention.

Jesus 'came into the world to save sinners' (see 1 Timothy 1.15). To save them from what? From the results of sin in the world, and from the sin in their own lives – which was and is a rejection of God's way. All sin is a form of rebellion against God.

Right from the beginning, as depicted in Genesis 3, there is the clear message that there is a 'being' behind sin, rather than simply a case of people making decisions on their own to do other than what we know as God's will.

Through the Old Testament there is far less than we might expect about the devil or Satan. We have the accounts in the Book of Job of course, which are very instructive. We have references in the Book of Daniel to opposition stopping God's messenger, and there are quite a lot of other instances. However it is not until we reach the New Testament that (if we can express it this way) we start to find Satan getting anxious.

Perhaps a key verse for us is 1 John 3:8b, 'The reason the Son of God appeared was to destroy the devil's work' (NIV). So taking our 'chrysalis' viewpoint we need to ask ourselves which incidents in the earthly ministry of Jesus speak about this, and how God demonstrates this aspect in Jesus.

First, our thoughts will go to the Temptation in the wilderness, then we will look at one of the occasions when Jesus confronted a case of spirit possession.

We start then at the beginning of Jesus' ministry, directly after that major and very public occasion of his baptism which we looked at in a previous chapter, and we recall the way in which the Holy Spirit showed himself and the Father spoke, and so was revealed something of the Holy Trinity. We are told next that Jesus was 'led by the Spirit' into the wilderness, there to be tempted by the devil, and it was over a period of forty days, although the only accounts come from the end of that period. It was as though the devil, who had succeeded with Adam, was being the chance to face the 'Second Adam', Jesus, with direct testing (for that is what the word temptation means). If he succeeded, then sin would have come into the life of the one person God sent to deal with the sin in other people's lives, and so the whole of God's plan would have been thwarted.

We notice at once that Satan did not work in the way he seems to work in relation to ordinary people, namely by the use of his messengers (yes, the Bible even calls them Satan's angels!) but instead he gave Jesus his own personal attention. It was a crucial occasion for both sides. For Jesus it was a question of whether his whole mission would break down on this one occasion when he was facing the full force of Satan in the way that any ordinary person would, and Satan was using the most subtle means he knew. For Satan there was the realisation that if he lost this 'round' he would find it very hard to break through at any other point, even though he tried. For both, to use modern idiom, it was a 'must win' encounter.

There is no need here to go into the details of the three temptations. It is sufficient to say that as and when a temptation comes, each is geared to attack what Satan sees as being a potentially vulnerable place, somewhere he had a chance of getting Jesus to do something, anything, that was not fulfilling God's plan and purpose. That would mean rebellion against God, which is the very nature of sin.

However, there is one point which we need to make: while God sees the whole picture in every situation and thus the future as well as the past, there is no reason at all to think that Satan has any foreknowledge. He can only attempt to trip people up or to respond to situations. That applied in the time of Jesus, and it also applies in our own lives. Knowing this can be a big comfort for us, and at times it can be something we can exploit as we resist Satan.

So Jesus had first to show that Satan was not able to trip him up. Jesus was aware of just what was going on. For our purpose here it does not matter whether we think that Satan appeared as a man to Jesus (there is certainly no scriptural basis for artistic portrayals such as a black-winged man or a being with horns) or whether it was Jesus just being aware of Satan's spiritual presence – which is the sort of thing that can happen to us.

When that period was over, and we are only told of three personal temptations at the end of the forty-day period of temptation in the wilderness so we can only surmise about what happened during the rest of the time, we are told that the devil left him for a period. Temptation would come again for Jesus, even if in less explicit ways, and will always do for us as well.

It was clearly God's plan that this monumental encounter should take place. It was needed in the mission and ministry of Jesus, and the fact that it happened has proved right through the centuries to be of the greatest help to Christians who have to face temptation as a result of their decision to go God's way in their own lives.

There is another aspect here that we can well look at in more detail before we move on. It is apparent as we look at the accounts of Jesus and his confrontations with Satan and his evil or 'unclean' spirits, and it is just as apparent today: as we have already mentioned there seem to be clear limits on Satan's knowledge – he responds to what happens rather than having foreknowledge or being able to know our thinking as contrasted with speaking or actions. So, in the life of Jesus, we see that Satan seems to have had the same expectations as the people of the time. While he recognised Jesus as the Son of God and therefore his major foe, he does not seem to have understood how Jesus was going to fulfil his role. If we look at the temptations in the wilderness, they seem to be directed towards Jesus being stopped from being the leader or king that the Jews expected their Messiah (God's anointed One) to be. The climax of the temptations was when Satan was almost saying: if you want to come and rule, you can do so subject to my being overlord, and that will cut out the hardship you are expecting in your life on earth.

Again, if we look ahead to the account of the Passion, we can read into it the thought that Satan may have had of stopping Jesus from being a king and winning the allegiance of the Jewish people – hence the betrayal, which was in fact the first step that has been prepared as a necessary commencement for the fulfilling of God's plan (which would be worked through in precise detail as we shall see later) for Jesus to go to the Cross and then rise from the dead.

Or look back: there was no attempt by Satan to prevent the birth of Jesus; he simply tried to respond after the event with the slaughter of the innocents at Bethlehem.

The devil may operate strategically today. Some years ago, we had a lady whose troubles were clearly pointing to some spirit troubling her and affecting her health. She was a person with a real Christian faith, a member of the church, and she belonged to a ladies' prayer group which met weekly. When we realised the situation, the suggestion was made that as we were going shortly to have a 'parish weekend' away at a Christian conference centre, we would use the opportunity of strong prayer support to seek God's deliverance for her. The plan was made and the enemy was aware of our plan because we discussed it. Directly we arrived at the place, she was taken ill – not badly but enough to keep her in her room, in bed. That continued from the Friday evening when we arrived until after lunch on the Sunday, then she was suddenly well enough for the journey home! So we said never mind, for there was another very suitable occasion coming up shortly (it might have been an area healing service, I cannot remember). This time the enemy tried the same trick only in a more elaborate way: he got her into hospital through her being taken ill again. But on visiting her in hospital I had the opportunity for a lot more listening to the full story and we became aware of what Satan or his minions were doing.

So this time I said nothing to her about any plan, but arranged with my wife, who was leading the little weekly prayer group to which she belonged, that I might call in at the end of their meeting that day. When I turned up, they asked why I had come. I said that it was for prayer with this one lady. They said they had already prayed for her. Immediately, I started a prayer concerning her being set free from this spirit – through the power of Jesus and acting in his name. Then there was a little noise from her (almost an 'Oh') and the spirit had gone. It was as though it had not known this time what had been planned.

Such a thought can be a great comfort to us, but it is also a warning that when the enemy sees something has happened to help forward our Christian lives, he is very likely to want to respond. Such has often been found with those who have responded to a gospel appeal at an evangelistic occasion, so much so that it has long been standard practice to warn people to expect temptations in the following few days. Many have also found it happening on returning home from a spiritually uplifting experience.

Now we can return to those occasions when Jesus faced an 'unclean' spirit in someone. There are plenty of such accounts, but we will centre on just one of them, in Luke chapter 8. Probably because Luke was a doctor, we often find more details of the healing stories in his Gospel than the others. But this one stands out.

Jesus had gone across to the eastern side of the Sea of Galilee, into an area that was not predominantly Jewish, and where the Jewish religious laws (such as those concerning the keeping and eating of pigs) were not observed by many of the people. He was met there by a demon-possessed man who was living wild and unable to mix in the community. Immediately he saw Jesus he shouted out, recognising who he was. Such is always the way with such spirits, they cannot bear even the name of Jesus because it is the name that speaks of their defeat.

It seems as though Jesus' immediate response was to order the spirit to leave the man, but that the spirit resisted at first. That rings true in modern situations, for where a spirit has had a 'nice home' for a long time within a person's life it will often fight to be able to stay there, and even more so when (as in this case) that person's life is a communal home for several spirits. It is interesting, too, to see that in the presence of Jesus the spirit 'broke cover' and was ordered to identify itself. This is what is often found in modern situations.

The spirit tried to bargain with Jesus, and what followed seems strange to us, with the spirits (for that is what they proved to be – they even called themselves 'legion' because there so many) asking to go into a herd of pigs nearby. We cannot know why Jesus allowed that, especially as it led directly to the herd taking fright and destroying themselves.

What we do notice is that the man concerned was totally transformed, and that the people around found that situation frightening. Again, that can happen today. I once had a woman whose husband (and she was preparing to divorce him because of his behaviour when under the influence of a spirit) complained to the bishop that he had been healed!

This is not the place to go into the story in detail and seek to learn all the lessons we can from it – our purpose is to ask why God allowed the account of the demoniac, and similar situations in several other recorded incidents, to appear in the Gospel accounts. Could it not be that Jesus had to be seen to be able not only to defeat Satan's attacks on his own life (in the Temptations) and thus be shown to be the 'last Adam' of whom Paul speaks in 1 Corinthians 15:45, but also to have the power to overcome other manifestations of Satan's activity. The devil's attacks are both direct and indirect (through unclean spirits) and the enemy's intention is to defeat God's purposes in the world.

We find in Luke's next chapter an incident which concerned a boy who had what we can recognise as epilepsy but which is spoken of as being a spirit. Probably both interpretations are right – there was an illness which we recognise, but at times illness (even if rarely) can have a link to sin, to evil. Sometimes this is because the illness has come about owing to actions which are against God's teaching and laws. Not often would there be a spirit involved, but I have experienced it in my own life as something inherited. We note that Jesus on at least one occasion told a person who had been healed to sin no more (see John 5:14; cp. also 8:11). This can also speak to us of the fact that sometimes guilt has to be dealt with, forgiveness experienced, before there can be a physical healing. Certainly Jesus brings together both aspects – and these are incidents where there is no outward sign of the presence of an evil spirit.

Perhaps at this point there should be given a clear warning that confronting a spirit presence, whether in a person's life or in a building, is not something to be done without being thoroughly prepared and trained for the work. There have been far too many cases where enthusiasm without knowledge and experience gained with those who have met such problems before has led to real problems.

So why do we have these accounts in the life of Jesus? Why did God plan for them to be recorded for us when there were so many incidents in his life that must have been unrecorded? Surely it is because Jesus had to be seen as having the power in himself, and not only because of what was to be seen through the Cross and resurrection to be the ultimate defeat of Satan's power. It was also so that we would grasp how we are to handle such problems when working in Jesus' name, as the final verses of Mark's Gospel show.

7

THE TRANSFIGURATION
See Matthew 17:2

As we come to the start of this chapter centring our thoughts on the Transfiguration, we are in a sense at the watershed within the ministry of Jesus. It is as though up to this point he has been fulfilling his role for the years of ministry, then from this point onwards the focus is far more centred on the Cross and the events that were to lead up to it, all of them fulfilling the purposes of God in a most wonderful way. We shall be looking at that aspect as we progress.

But first it would be good to bring together those subjects we have been considering so far. It is all too easy to get so immersed in the details that we lose sight of the broader picture of what we are really about, and that is seeing the overall plan of God for revealing himself, in Jesus, both to the people amongst whom he lived, and through what was written down under the guidance of the Holy Spirit for us too, so many generations on from there.

Our first chapter was speaking of the danger of seeing the plans of God simply from our human standpoint, looking at the details in the ministry of Jesus as we read and understand them and learning from what have become very well-known and much loved incidents. There is the danger of picking-and-choosing in these so as to centre on the things we find easy, things we feel are helpful or beautiful and which are setting an example for us. But I felt a need to see which incidents most clearly signal God's agenda and purposes in Jesus Christ. (Though of course it must always be remembered that the *whole* of Scripture does this, and it is *all* profitable for teaching.) To put it another way, I feel that the slightly more detached viewpoint which has come to me in the 'chrysalis' phase of life, with more of an ability to look at the whole rather than just one incident at a time – and this has been a time of starting to feel a bit detached from the ordinary concerns of church life, and it has been a stage of getting ready for the life beyond – has helped me to discern more about God's purposes revealed in Scripture.

Our next chapter centred upon the Incarnation and the things that surrounded that most wonderful event when God became man, 'for us and for our salvation'. We have tried to see the way that the series of individual events, from the angelic appearance to Zechariah in the Temple, through to the coming of the magi to Bethlehem (an event that may well have been a year or so after the birth of Jesus) fit together as a coherent whole. In that sequence we saw how there were several occasions when God 'broke into' the ordinary life of those involved, with amazing angelic visitations and visions so that there could be no doubt about the momentous nature, as well as the meaning, of what was happening. Here was God 'making all the moves', following his own plan, and letting just a few people in on that plan – and those not the sort of people whom we might have expected to be included in it.

We moved on into the 'silent years'. We looked in detail at the one story we have from the boyhood period of Jesus' earthly life, the incident in the Temple when he was twelve years old, and we saw from that how he was clearly aware of his divine purpose. It raised the question of how we are to look at his divinity and his humanity, and the danger of so stressing the humanity of Jesus that we lose sight of the things that point out to us the extent to which divinity was not something that came to him at a later stage but was there from the beginning. Even though we then hear nothing until he was in (at least) his late twenties, and had been living and working as an ordinary tradesman in a somewhat despised village in Galilee, he had been fulfilling God's plan of his living fully, in great humility, the life of an ordinary Jew – we could say an 'observant Jew' – of that period (and let us never forget that Jesus was a Jew). We saw that Jesus had come not just to 'do' but very much to 'be'. He was tested as a man, with temptations that come to man, over a prolonged period. It is worth remembering that while of course there were the exceptions (and we hear of some of these) life expectancy for ordinary folk of those days would have been nothing like as long as for us. So by the time he embarked upon his ministry, Jesus was probably well over half way through a normal life expectancy and would have been seen as a mature man.

From there we moved to the next huge event, the baptism of Jesus. We saw that repentance was not just a looking back, but equally a looking ahead with dedication. In complete humility, Jesus took that step, as people were turning to God with expectation that something very important was about to happen and thus sought to be ready by (re)dedicating themselves to obedience to his way and his law.

Yet something spoken of in the preaching of both John the Baptist and Jesus at that time was not quite what had been expected. They preached the coming of the kingdom of heaven (Matthew) or the kingdom of God (Mark and Luke). The people expected a messiah-king to lead the nation, and in that to bring back independence from the dominance of a foreign power, most recently Rome. But that was not the sort of kingdom that God intended at that time.

Then we looked at the message of Jesus. It centred not

on the Jewish people being set free from Rome but on the building up in the community of 'colonies of heaven's kingdom' as the followers of Jesus became members of his kingdom. His preaching of the way of life set out in the Sermon on the Mount, and in many other places, particularly the parables of the kingdom, was there for us to follow as members of that kingdom. He spoke of the kingdom being 'within' or 'among' you, a kingdom of allegiance to him and to God's way while living in ordinary society.

We also had to see the confrontation between Jesus and the powers of darkness, how he faced Satan in the direct Temptations in the wilderness, and through the meeting with people in whom some form of unclean or evil spirit presence had become a reality.

Let us link these together in a simple series of words: humility and living as man amongst ordinary people; identification even to the point of sharing in temptation and yet without sin; teaching the ways of God; and we can add, even though we have not explored it in detail, the showing forth of the love and care of God for the whole of people's lives through his healing ministry. Such then was the main direction over the greater part of his three years of ministry, but it was a ministry that had not as yet come to face the greatest issue, dealing with 'the sin of the world' even though John the Baptist had announced him as coming to do just that (and we can notice that he spoke of Jesus as the Lamb of God, rather than announcing Jesus as the expected Messiah).

It is at that point therefore that we turn our thoughts and attention to the Transfiguration, which again we are very familiar with and often draw lessons from. But do we think enough as to why it happened, and why it was clearly planned by God to happen at that point?

However perhaps first we need to think about something that does not often get much attention, namely the loneliness and stress that Jesus must have experienced during his ministry. Many are only too aware of how those in a 'top position', whether in business, government or elsewhere, can feel lonely and isolated. There is the thought that 'the buck stops here', and there is nobody over them or to whom they report, even if there is a committee or board who make strategic decisions. In everyday affairs they are the ones who have to take the action. They can seek advice but that is as far as it goes. It can apply in business, and even the minister of a church can feel something of this. Yet, when we think of Jesus, somehow we pay little attention to his own emotions, and to the stress that he must have experienced. He was unique, being divine and being completely man. He would have been aware of the nature and presence of sin in a way that nobody else was. He would have known that he had been sent into the world with the huge mission of starting – and by his actions on the Cross to enable – the whole plan for the redemption of the world, and of setting up colonies of God's kingdom. Is it any wonder with that load that we hear of times when he was overcome by tiredness when the disciples weren't? Think of the way he was left alone by the well at Samaria while the disciples went to get food, because he was weary (John 4:6), also the time when he was asleep in the boat in a dangerous storm (Matthew 8:24).

Yet all through the first part of his ministry, even when he had chosen the Twelve, did Jesus declare openly to them who he was? He 'dropped hints' every time he worked a miracle, and he gave what was clearly unique teaching, His whole manner of life which they saw so closely was pointing in a certain direction. But no direct statement, for he clearly wanted, and the Father's plan was for this, that they were to reach the conclusion by working things out through their minds rather than some spectacular demonstration or vision of his glorious, heavenly nature – until this moment.

In a sense such seems to be the case today. God lets people reach their own conclusions about the person and nature of Jesus through what they hear and read, through personal thinking, through what is seen in the life of other people. What we call 'spiritual experiences' in which Jesus seems particularly close to us are usually experienced after a point of belief and commitment to being Christ's and being a member of his kingdom has been reached.

It was this point that has just been reached with the Twelve immediately before the Transfiguration, when Jesus put the question to them as to who he was, while they were at Caesarea Philippi, an area well to the north of the Sea of Galilee, up the Jordan valley and on the fringe of the Jewish area. There Peter spoke up for all the others, stating "You are the Christ, the Son of the living God" (Matthew 16:16). You could say that they had reached what we might call a 'conversion' moment, when their belief and faith were expressed outwardly. Jesus had fulfilled that part of his objective. It was to lead on to the most amazing spiritual experience that any Christians have had, which we call the Transfiguration.

Where did it happen? All we are told is that Jesus led the three closest disciples, Peter, James and John, up a high mountain by themselves. Traditionally this has always been thought of as Mount Tabor in Galilee, an isolated mountain in the flatter area of the country. Perhaps an alternative would be somewhere in the area of Mount Hermon. That would be farther from population, and being already at Caesarea Philippi they were not too far from there. However, it is not the place that really matters much, rather we need to think of other aspects.

We are not told whether it was during the daytime that Jesus was so wonderfully transfigured into what was approaching his (normal before the Incarnation) heavenly glory. The only clue the accounts give is a dazzling light. But we need to ask ourselves, without any possibility of a clear answer, as to whether this was a one-off event or something that happened for Jesus from time to time but was only witnessed by any of his followers on this occasion. We know that he seems to have had the practice of going at times to spend a night, to have a longer time, in solitary prayer and communication with his Father, as for instance in Mark 1:35. So when that happened did he become transfigured? Then again we wonder how long the experience that the three disciples witnessed lasted – whether it was a matter of minutes or over a period of hours, for it seems that the disciples dropped off to sleep while it was happening (Luke 9:32) – something we can compare with what happened at Gethsemane later.

This all leads us to think about the significance of this event (which Peter writes about in 2 Peter 1:16–18, clearly showing the impression it had made upon them). We need to think of it in terms of its purpose in the life of Jesus, its purpose for the three disciples, and for the Twelve who would clearly have been told about it, even though it was not to be widely known. We need to think about its purpose for us too.

Why did it happen at this point in the ministry of Jesus? The Father's voice had been heard at the start of Jesus' ministry, at his baptism; it was also heard here and at one further point, when encouragement was clearly needed, during the final week in Jerusalem, as recorded in John 12:28. In each instance, therefore, the voice came at a significant point when that support was needed.

Here we are at a very real watershed point. It seems that from now onwards Jesus saw his Galilean ministry being largely finished and he starts to turn his thoughts, his direction, towards Jerusalem and the prospect of the Cross. He seems to have started at once to prepare the Twelve for the events that were to come at Jerusalem. It was turning from ministry and the setting up of the colonies of the kingdom of heaven, towards mission and the main purpose for which he came, namely going to the Cross and then rising from the dead.

So we are told how, in this experience, Moses and Elijah met with Jesus and the Father's voice was heard. Moses the lawgiver and Elijah, who was always seen as one of the greatest prophets of the Old Testament (even though we do not have a written record of his teaching), thus represented 'the Law and the Prophets' which was the division that the Jews made, and make, between two parts of the Old Testament. Here then were two key figures from the past, men whose own end of life experiences were both out of the normal (Moses, we are told, was buried by God on Mt. Pisgah – Deuteronomy 34; Elijah was taken up to heaven in a chariot of fire – 2 Kings 2:11) but whose presence together spoke of the oneness of the Old Testament, and thus of Jesus as being linked directly to what had been going on and the way that God had revealed himself in the past centuries. These two men came to talk to Jesus about what was going to happen at Jerusalem, towards which Jesus was now going to be setting his direction – both literally and also in terms of his purposes.

So for Jesus himself here was a wonderful moment for being reassured, for being encouraged, for getting things into perspective even, with all the hardness of the road ahead of him, of being spiritually strengthened. We can be sure that it was the purpose of the Father for that to happen, and it all goes to emphasise the humanity of Jesus. How easily we forget that he would have had a man's emotions. It would have been especially hard for him, knowing far more than we would about the pain which was to come.

For the three who witnessed the Transfiguration, here was

the confirmation of what they had come to believe about Jesus. They were given a glimpse of his heavenly glory. They were assured that he was the one whom they had declared and believed him to be. They saw him in his full glory, and thus his heavenly importance within the divine plan, even if they did not yet fully grasp yet the implications about the death that he had started to talk about directly after Peter's great confession at Caesarea Philippi, which might have been days or a week or two beforehand. We can see clearly why it was that it came to be recorded in the Gospels.

But how about for ourselves, and the reasons for us that it was written down? We see it as a very important milestone in the life of Jesus. It is the clearest indication that we can have of his wonderful nature, and that the Jesus we read of in the Gospels is one and the same with the Lord of whom we read, in his full heavenly glory, in the Book of Revelation – especially in Revelation 1:12–end and 5:6–end.

It also brings a challenge for us in our worship, for it is far too easy to worship and to pray only thinking of Jesus as the man of Galilee, the one who has known, experienced and thus understands what life is like for us. We need to be able to get the vision of his glory. To quote from a chorus that was popular a few years ago, we need to 'worship his majesty'.

But there is something more that is very important for us to grasp. When the voice came on that Mount of Transfiguration it had a command. That command we can be sure was not just to the three (or the Twelve) who were doing it already. It said 'Listen to him.' In this, he was speaking to us. It is easy to think of the example of Jesus and the way he portrayed God's love in action; it is something different to grasp that it is a command for us to listen to (or perhaps we should say now, to read carefully and take note of) the teaching of Jesus. Jesus said "You call me Teacher and Lord, and rightly so, for that is what I am" (John 13:13). It is something that we can easily talk about, but do we really put it into practice? For the command to us to come at such a significant moment in the ministry of Jesus can only reinforce its importance for us.

Whether or not Jesus had similar experiences of closeness to the Father, with or without the 'glory', is something we do not need to know. To meet with Moses and Elijah was clearly a 'one-off'. There can be no doubting that this was indeed another of the vital stages with deep truths to teach us, which God the Holy Spirit, working in the lives of the Evangelists, planned to be recorded.

It might be worthwhile stopping to think over what we would lack from our Christian understanding and in the outworking of our own Christian lives if that event had been without the three there – without, therefore, being recorded for us. How amazing it is that such a very intimate experience between Jesus and the Father should have been 'deliberately leaked' as we would say today, for us to learn from.

8

THE FINAL WEEK
See John 12:1, 12–16

We can often look at a passage in the Gospels, especially if we feel that we know it well, and take the wider picture rather than think much about individual words that might at first glance seem insignificant. But in doing that we may find that we are missing some of what we might call the 'finer points' of the message. It is with one of those that we start this chapter.

In modern translations of the Gospels we often find the Greek word *hora* translated as 'time'; in the Authorised Version it is translated as 'hour', and that is the correct meaning. We can look at many other instances in the New Testament that show it being used of a precise time and hour, rather than in a general way to speak of a wider period.

John tells us that Jesus said to Mary that his hour had not come yet (see John 2:4). He also speaks of a time that is coming and has now come, in response to the woman at the well of Samaria (see John 4:23) and timing ("is coming and has now come") again comes to the fore at John 5:25, in relation to the "dead" who will hear, and the life which is in Jesus, and Jesus' authority as Son of Man to judge.

But then we go to the final night of Jesus' life – first in the Upper Room, in the account of the foot washing (John 13:1), and again in the opening of what we call the High

Priestly Prayer (17:1ff), we find Jesus speaking of how the 'hour' had come.

As we go forward and look at what happened in the final week of the Lord's life, and try to see how the plan of the Father was being fulfilled, the message stands out clearly that whatever the Lord was going through, the precise details of God's plan were being fulfilled so that there could be no mistake as to the meaning – and one of those details concerns the timing.

While we look in this chapter more at the start of the week, we see that the timing mattered then. Later on in the account, even the hour at which things happened really mattered, so that when Paul speaks of how Christ our Passover Lamb was sacrificed for us (see 1 Corinthians 5:7) he was doing this in the knowledge that what Jesus did on the Cross coincided with the sacrificing of the Passover lambs in the Temple. We will come to look later at the way that worked out, but for the moment we want to see how the events that led up to the crucifixion had been carefully planned so the full significance was there.

Many speak today as though the events of that week somehow occurred because of the way in which the authorities, the crowds, and Jesus with his group of disciples had happened to respond to one another. They look at it all from the standpoint of human thinking. The authorities clearly were finding Jesus an embarrassing problem, the crowds were responding to what happened, the rulers of the Jews were seeking above all to keep the peace with the Roman occupying army, so that the special way of life and worship that the Jews were allowed was not in any way upset. It is seen by some as though circumstances led to responses, and thus, stage by stage, things just happened – all a matter of people responding to other people, and somehow the plan of God was being worked out through what happened so that

Jesus was crucified, and that opened the way for the action of God in the greatest miracle of the resurrection.

But is that point of view, seeing everything from a very human standpoint, really the correct way of looking at it? As we try to see things more from the divine perspective, perhaps one of the most amazing things of all is that the plan of God was worked out, especially at the end, not just to get the right season of the year, or even the right week or day for things to happen, but even down to the actual hour fitting in with the plan. More than that, we can see how the very words of Jesus at the very end of his time on the Cross also fitted exactly. It all fills our minds with an ever greater sense of the wonder of what God was doing through all of this, and as it does it heightens in us a sense of worship. Men sinned, but God was working to overrule so that his amazing plan, the plan made in love but fulfilled at the greatest possible cost, was fulfilled.

We need to go back to the start of that week. It would seem that Jesus planned his journey, in which not just the group of his disciples and other followers travelled together, but probably they linked up with the groups from a wide area who were all converging on Jerusalem for the greatest Feast in the Jewish calendar. It was planned for a time when all Jews who were able to make the journey (mostly on foot, but some coming by sea from other countries) were supposed to be at Jerusalem. In that planning, he may well have made the journey up from Jericho on the Friday, a walk that would have been physically hard as it was through a desert region and involved a climb of several hundred feet on a rocky path in conditions of considerable heat.

Then we may well surmise that he went to his friends Lazarus, Martha and Mary in the village of Bethany to spend the Sabbath (Friday evening to Saturday evening). In fact he probably had at least two nights there.

It was thus on the Sunday morning (the day we call Palm Sunday) that Jesus then made the final journey of two or three miles to Jerusalem. We are all very familiar with the story which we are told in the four Gospels (it is one of the few stories that is found in all of them). But let us try to think more of what actually happened.

The impression in the Gospels is of a crowd centring round Jesus, the thought of him riding on the donkey making it all very obvious. But was it really such a big event? If it had been the huge event that Christians often mentally surmise, we can imagine that it would have caused alarm not just with the Jewish leaders but with the Roman authorities, in the way that happened years later when there was a threat to peace when Paul was arrested in the Temple (Acts 21:30–32). The Roman commander then took immediate action with a contingent of soldiers. Surely such a large event on what we call Palm Sunday would have provoked a Roman response? But there is no sign of any such thing happening either in the Gospels or in contemporary records.

So we should probably think in terms of how many excited parties of pilgrims were arriving every day, and especially on that day, with singing and shouting, often singing the pilgrim songs we call the 'Songs of Ascents', Psalms 120 – 134. It was what happened every year, and the authorities expected it. So outwardly this was just one group, however large it was, amongst many others. Over this period there were many thousands arriving and then camping in the surrounding area. We read of some of the Pharisees being in the crowd and being anxious over what was happening. Probably we don't need to think of a group hurriedly coming out of the city, but rather that some Pharisees were in the pilgrim parties, for they lived all over the country and would be amongst those more anxious to attend the Feast.

But why did Jesus choose that day to arrive at Jerusalem,

and then, when he arrived, go straight to the Temple before leaving to go back to Bethany for the night? Why all the 'publicity' of his arrival, only to return quietly to the same place?

The answer must surely lie in two Old Testament passages. The first is in the instructions for the keeping of the Passover in Exodus 12. Each family or group of families was to choose a lamb sufficient for the needs of that number of people, but they were not to go out on the morning of the day on which they would be celebrating the Passover meal in the evening to get it and have it slaughtered ready for the meal. They were told that they were to choose the lamb several days before (on the tenth day) and yet not slaughter it until the fourteenth day of the month. It was therefore to be kept by – become almost part of – the family for those few days, before it was killed as a sacrifice. Such a procedure would help the people to realise that it was being offered on their behalf, something that would bring home the seriousness of what was being done, and not just have the emphasis on the celebration of the feast.

So, on the right day before the Passover, Jesus 'our Passover', the 'Lamb of God who takes away the sin of the world', arrived. Not only so, but he did what had to be done with the lambs: they had to be taken to the Temple to be checked over and approved. So Jesus went straight to the Temple. He even went to the area where lambs were being sold (and presumably also checked by the priests), for it was there that he objected to the Temple outer 'court of the Gentiles' being used for a market.

It was all tying in with getting his 'hour' right. How wonderfully God was ensuring that everything was fitting together. But there was another aspect, too. We read in John 12:16 that when the disciples cut palm branches and threw down their cloaks for Jesus on the donkey to ride over, they did not realise that they were fulfilling the prophecy in Zechariah 9:9 about the arrival of God's King. They thought they were acting spontaneously to honour Jesus, but they were doing what had been foretold centuries earlier.

We can see here again the hand of God. That arrival gave the nation the chance to accept their God-sent Messiah to be the kind of King which God had planned. They passed the opportunity over, rejecting him. To this day, the orthodox Jews continue to reject Jesus. But the wonder is that God was able to overrule what had happened and the events linked to it, so that the greater plan for the salvation of the world could be fulfilled.

However, for a moment we need to take some steps back in the narrative, in fact perhaps over a period of months, although we find it very hard to piece together any sort of accurate timetable, for the Gospels did not set out to do that. There is a tendency to think of what Jesus was doing, and not to think of what it all meant to him.

One thing that has come over already in our studies is that Jesus did not lose divinity when he became man, he brought both aspects of his person together, and that for the whole of his life. Again and again the little incidents fit into place when we accept this very basic truth. But yet, he was man with all that entailed, including thoughts, feelings and emotions, and it was all made more difficult for him by the fact that although he had several times over this period since the Transfiguration sought to explain to his close followers, the Twelve, what was going to happen, they had clearly not wanted to hear and understand. Such a thought was too much for them to cope with.

Those of us who have at some period in our lives had to face something very unpleasant, such as going to hospital for a serious operation, know how much it helps to have the moral support of family and friends who understand our feelings, fears, apprehensions as far as anyone is able to. But it would seem that this just did not happen for Jesus; they saw him with a sense of purpose and direction and realised no doubt that he was troubled, that he was perhaps not 'the same' as he had been when travelling around Galilee in the early days. He had to carry his thoughts, and the burden of the sins of the world, alone. Our thoughts may turn to Isaiah 63:3 and see that as a prophecy of what was to happen not just at the Cross but right through this period.

We can think of the words in Luke 9:51 "As the time approached for him to be taken up to heaven, Jesus resolutely (AV = stedfastly) set out for Jerusalem ..." Perhaps we can picture in our minds a look of resolution, stepping out with determination rather than a relaxed approach to walking and talking.

Then notice that there are two occasions when we are told of Jesus weeping, and often tears can be a sign not only of sadness but also stress. The first is at the grave of Lazarus at Bethany, yet that was when he knew he had gone there to take away their sorrow and raise Lazarus (John 11:35); he had seemingly gone there from the comparative safety of the Jordan valley. The second occasion was during the Palm Sunday procession (if we can call it that) from Bethany to Jerusalem – when the city came into view as he went down the pathway (for that is what their roads were) from the top of the Mount of Olives, diagonally across the front of the hill towards Gethsemane and the journey up the other side to the city. As Jesus first saw the city he wept over it knowing what was going to happen there some forty years later, when after a terrible siege the beautiful city and Temple would be totally destroyed and many would lose their lives in a time of awful suffering.

Or we can think of the time when, as his feet were being anointed during a meal in Bethany (was that just before Palm

Sunday?), he spoke of it as being a preparation for his burial. Clearly he was well aware of what was going to happen.

Jesus carried that mental and emotional burden alone because nobody could grasp either what was going to happen, or really see the wonder of the plan of God that was being worked out. Yet, remembering what we are told in Matthew 9:4, Jesus clearly understood the inner thoughts of all those around him even if they were unable to grasp even the main direction of where he was going.

Perhaps the Twelve got a little nearer to that when, remembering what he had said on the way into Jerusalem and also what he had said to them when in the Temple about how the magnificent building, then not fully complete after forty years of refurbishment, extension and improvement, was going to be destroyed, they had come to him a day or two later (during that final week) while again on the Mount of Olives – maybe on their daily journey to and from Bethany – and asked him when all the dire things he had described would be fulfilled. Jesus gave us what we call the 'little Apocalypse' which we find in Matthew 24 (and parallels in Mark and Luke). Clearly he had the knowledge in detail, and spoke not just about the events of AD 70, but also looking right ahead to things that are still in the future for us. (Such double signification can sometimes be found in prophecy.)

We could go more fully into the details of that final week, but such is not our purpose here – our concern is to grasp how God's amazing plan was being fulfilled by the Lord, who was fully aware of that plan and of the cost it would be to him personally. We need to see how it was the eternal plan, made by the Father and the Son, brought to fruition as the precise point in the history of the world that God saw to be the best, and worked out in one generation amongst the countless generations of people who have lived in the world.

God chose that period in the history of the Jewish nation

and we can see some of the reasons for his choice. It was at a time when there was an expectation amongst the Jews and a looking for their Messiah to save and redeem them (even if their expectation was different from God's plan). It was a period when under the rule of Rome there was an acceptance of the Jewish strongly held monotheism (worshipping only one god) which meant that Christianity, seen at first by the Roman authorities as a sect within Judaism, could be established. During that period, travel was comparatively safe as Rome had established a rule of law throughout the Mediterranean area, dealt with the pirates who had made sea travel very dangerous, and had established a system of roads. All this enabled the new faith to be established in the period before the destruction of the Temple in AD 70.

Here then was Jesus, so fully aware of what was happening, and knowing the cost not just to himself but to the Father as well, 'treading [that] winepress alone'. How easy it is for us to centre our thinking just on the physical suffering of Jesus, terrible though that was, and not even attempt to grasp that he was bearing the mental anguish not only of sin, but also of having all the burden placed on him while those around were not able to share it with him.

> "Is it nothing to you, all you who pass by?
> Look around and see.
> Is any suffering like my suffering
> that was inflicted on me,
> that the LORD brought on me
> in the day of his fierce anger?"
>
> *Lamentations 1:12, NIV*

9

THE LAST SUPPER
See Matthew 26:17–19, 26–29

There is hardly any Christian denomination that does not make what is most usually called the Holy Communion its most important regular act of worship, for all are seeking to obey their Lord's instruction "Do this in remembrance of me." Some have the service on a daily basis, others will make sure there is a weekly opportunity for their members to participate. There are others that make it very special by having it only monthly or quarterly, even making it an annual event on the evening of Maundy Thursday. There are those who want to make it something so important in acknowledging that all Christians are part of one faith that they welcome any baptised believer. For very similar reasons there are churches that make it special by limiting those who can take part to their own members. Some make it an occasion for both ceremonial and symbolic actions whilst others want to keep it very simple, feeling that this was how it was when Jesus gave us this action as a way of being a memorial of him.

We call it by all sorts of names too, ranging from the mass to 'the breaking of bread'. We find it called the Eucharist (from a Greek word meaning thanksgiving), the Holy Communion, the Lord's Supper, even 'the sacrament' although that ignores the other 'sacrament of the gospel' or dominical sacrament (meaning ordained by the Lord, by

Jesus), namely baptism. Whatever the name, it centres round the breaking of bread and poured out wine, of which those present (or sometimes only some of them) then partake.

If you ask any member of any church, they will probably be able to tell you that it was something Jesus told his followers to do. The majority are also likely to be able to tell you that it was given to the church by Jesus on the last night of his earthly life before he went to the Cross.

But if you ask them what was the occasion in the Jewish religious calendar when it happened, you would probably be met by a blank stare! Yet it was the occasion on which it happened, with all the meaning that had for those present, which is vital for our understanding not just of the meaning of the service but also for so much of our grasp of how the Old and New Testaments fit together.

Putting this in another way: if Jesus simply wanted a farewell meal with his friends as he knew he would be going to the Cross on the next day, surely he could have suggested that it was held at the place where we think he and perhaps all of them were staying – the home of Lazarus, Martha and Mary in Bethany. He was going there every evening during that week after teaching in the Temple and it would have been so much easier. But probably the thought never entered either his thoughts or those of the disciples, for they asked where he wanted them to make the necessary preparations.

The one place where all Jews tried to be for the Passover meal was in Jerusalem. The meat used was always lamb, and the lamb was part of a sacrifice that had been killed and offered in the Temple. Each family had a lamb, or perhaps we should say each group of families, for lamb was very expensive (especially at Passover time) and so each person would only have a very small portion of the meat in their meal, perhaps as small as an olive.

What is very clear is that Jesus intended that meal to be

the Passover celebration, yet that leaves us with one or two questions that Christians have tried to answer in various ways. As we read the accounts in the four Gospels, it seems that the Jews were observing the Passover on the evening of the Friday (what we would call Good Friday), yet that was after Jesus had died on the Cross. So how do we account for Jesus and his disciples celebrating it a day early? There are some who think that there is a muddle here, that the Passover was celebrated on the Thursday, yet that does not tie in with the words and actions of the Jewish leaders during the trial of Jesus or while he was on the Cross, but probably the answer lies in the fact that sometimes it was observed over two days, for it all depended upon when the new moon had been seen which marked out the beginning of the first month of the religious year – Nisan. Sometimes, therefore, you got people not all observing it on the same day.

There is another unusual aspect, too. From what we gather from the accounts we are given in the Gospels and by Paul in 1 Corinthians 11, there were just Jesus and his 'family' of the Twelve present, yet the normal thing was for as many of a person's natural family as possible to gather. It was rather like the way our families gather for a Christmas lunch or a major family occasion. We know that both Jesus and John had family members present in the Jerusalem area, yet the implications of what happened in the record of that evening make it apparent that they were not there. Clearly Jesus wanted something else very special, and that meant it needed to be with the Twelve together. We also note that when Paul was writing to the Christians in Corinth and described what happened, he never mentioned the Passover aspect, but then he was writing to a church that was almost entirely non-Jewish, for whom the Passover would have meant very little. This, however, was probably the first of the four accounts of the institution of the Communion to be written down. We need to note, too, that John, while telling very much more about that evening, never mentions the institution of the Communion, presumably because he was writing to supplement what had been written already.

So why is all this talk about the Passover important? The tendency in the churches in our generation is to have much thought and teaching based on different aspects of meaning that are in this most wonderful meal, celebration, form of worship. Some (and this links back to the names for the service) put the stress on remembering – using the words Jesus used – or commemoration of what he did on the Cross, with an emphasis on the cost. Others put the stress on thanksgiving for God's love in giving Jesus and on the thought therefore of the cost of our redemption, often linking it to the theme of Incarnation. Again, there can be a stress on the word 'covenant' which Jesus used, and thus on the fact that we have accepted a special relationship which demands our love and loyalty to him. Or there are those who put emphasis on the feeding of our spiritual lives upon Jesus (thinking of how he spoke of himself as being the 'bread of life'). All these aspects are completely right, all are needed, and we are correct to stress every one of them.

But we are looking at this from our 'chrysalis' viewpoint – so we ask what God was saying. Just as we asked why Jesus felt that he must be in Jerusalem and in the setting of the Passover to institute this memorial meal, so we are looking for an answer in the link that is in the message of the Passover itself, and the way that Jesus made changes in what was the traditional wording used then (and which has seen comparatively little alteration by Orthodox Jews to this day). Perhaps looking at some parts of the Passover meal will help us grasp what Jesus did, and why he did it.

The overall purpose of the meal for Jews in the time of Jesus, and right through to the present day, is to celebrate what God did in bringing the nation of Israel into existence, by redeeming, leading them out of Egypt through a display of his power, bringing them through the Red Sea to an independent existence, and then leading them to Sinai where he gave them his law through Moses and established his special relationship with them based on a covenant. The word 'covenant' is important, for it is the way that God sets up his relationship with people. He did it with Noah, he did it with Abraham, he did it with Israel at Sinai. It speaks of a legally-binding agreement, where the 'doing' is on one side with the other side accepting, as against a business transaction where the doing is on both sides, such as one providing the goods or services and the other agreeing to provide money in payment. It is linked to something outward and visible – the rainbow with Noah, circumcision with Abraham, sacrifice with Moses and the people of Israel. It is like God giving a gift (e.g. promises to Abraham about fathering a nation) and the other side accepting the relationship that has been set up with an agreement to keep to what has been laid down. Thus Israel became God's people because of what he had done for them, agreeing to obey his laws and fulfil his purposes for them.

So, in having the annual Passover meal, the nation and the people in it individually were reaffirming their special covenant relationship with God. It was (and still is) an annual reminder of who they were, and it should lead to a renewal of their commitment to keep the covenant God had given.

So the 'meal' was more than sitting down to eat. To this day there is first a little ceremonial eating of token food that reminds those present of the hardships the nation endured in Egypt (and, all the way through, the leader speaks as though those present had actually been part of the company who came out of Egypt – he speaks of 'us' not 'them'). Then there is a long recital of the history of the nation from the time of the call of Abraham right through to the exodus from Egypt and the journey to Sinai. It is told as a story, symbolically in answer to a child's question (and the youngest boy present is traditionally chosen to ask it) about why they are holding this meal. This can take a long time, perhaps a hour or more, but nobody is in any hurry. We are not told of Jesus, who was acting as the 'father in the family' on that evening, doing this but we can be reasonably sure that he would have done so.

But even before that recounting of history there would have been some other things happening. In the meal there were several ceremonial 'cups' when everybody's cup was filled with wine and all drank together. The first such was called the 'cup of sanctification' on the theme of "I will bring you out". There would also have been the foot washing, for all present had walked there over dusty unpaved roads, and sitting close together in a reclining position there would have been the risk of smelly feet (!). How this ties in with the story in John 13, when Jesus himself did what would usually be undertaken by a servant or (foreign) slave, but there was no such person present, and none of the disciples wanted to stoop to perform such a humble a task.

Another very important thing also took place – and still takes place, before the telling of the story. It was when the dish with all the tokens of the suffering in Egypt was uncovered, and one of the pieces of bread was broken. The leader traditionally says: "This is the bread of affliction which our ancestors ate in the land of Egypt...." Was it at that point that Jesus very markedly changed the words to "This is my body which is given for you..." or was it a little later (but still before they ate their meal)? The accounts which we have don't make it clear – the one thing that is stressed is that the time when Jesus gave them the cup was 'after supper', so after the meal, thus giving the thought that the first special action, the breaking and giving of the bread, was before the meal in this very long preliminary part of the evening.

Assuming then that the phrase 'This is my body' was spoken in the place where normally the leader would say 'This is the bread of affliction which your father ate in the land of Egypt', the traditional words when the unleavened bread was broken at this point, it would tend to put the emphasis for us as we receive the bread at the Communion upon grasping the suffering that Jesus went through for us. It makes us realise the cost of our salvation at the price of his broken body, as well as grasping through this as much as we can of the wonder of God's love being made known – manifested – through Jesus undergoing the whole path from Incarnation to the Cross, and especially the cost, both physical and spiritual, of bearing our sins in his own body.

Then, if this is correct, the 'cup' (one of the four during the meal when all shared) that became linked to the Communion would have been the one soon after the meal – that was called the 'cup of redemption'. Thus the two parts of what we have as a sacrament when the two are brought together would have been separated by the meal. This cup was followed by a psalm. Psalm 136 is often used today, and we are told in Matthew 26:30 that, 'When they had sung a hymn, they went out to the Mount of Olives' (NIV). But perhaps seeing where this comes, as distinct from the bread, helps us put the emphasis (as we receive the cup in the Communion) on the words that Jesus used at this point: 'This is my blood of the new covenant'. If the bread speaks of the cost to Jesus, the cup speaks of our commitment, or if we want to put it in this way, the cost of being committed to Jesus – but more of that later.

An alternative is that the giving of the bread was much later, just before the wine, but if this was the case why stress that the wine was given after the meal? We can also try to link this in to the story of the betrayal and the departure of Judas. The indications we are given point towards that taking place at the beginning of the meal, so if we are right about the dividing of the two aspects of the giving of the bread and the cup, he would have been there for the bread but not for the cup. Many feel that both took place after he had left, but much of this depends on the giving of the 'sop' (or special small morsel of food) to Judas, and whether that was linked to a particular point in the meal when a favoured person was given one by the leader, or whether Jesus made this incident an 'extra' and not part of the traditional order for the Passover meal.

For our purposes here these details are not of great concern – what we need to focus on as we look at this from our 'chrysalis' viewpoint is that the plan of God was so clearly to bring the Last Supper, on the final night of the Lord's life, right into the setting of the Passover. It was a way, perhaps the very best way possible, to link together the message of Jesus and his whole life with the overall message of the Old Testament. The Passover was speaking of redemption from Egypt, it was speaking of the setting up of the nation and therefore of beginnings. It was speaking of the nation of Israel being made God's special people who were to be under a covenant to live according to God's ways, and whose obedience was linked to the removal of sin through the shedding of blood with the sacrifice of animals.

Earlier we were thinking of the theme of setting up colonies of God's kingdom, and how the message of Jesus was showing – to both the disciples and to all generations of Christians – the ways, the laws we might call them, of that kingdom, as well as illustrating the principles through the 'parables of the kingdom'.

Now we see that Jesus is setting up a new covenant relationship, not to be based on the blood of sacrifices but upon his own blood being shed through the giving of his life upon the Cross. In doing this he was fulfilling what had been prophesied in Jeremiah 31:31–34, that God would set up a new covenant, initially with Israel, to replace the old one which had been broken so many times. How fitting that Jesus should do this, and giving the memorial meal was also to be a permanent reminder of the nature of our relationship with God, in the setting of the annual covenant meal of the Passover.

The message that comes from this to us as Christians seems very clear. All too often, many of us speak of 'going to Communion' in quite a casual way. Is it really thought through and prepared for – as going to an act of worship and seeking from that to draw near to God, worship him and be strengthened for our Christian witness? How often do we put the stress on all the obligations that come from making that meal a renewal of our pledge to belong to Jesus, to make him the Lord and Master of our lives, to live always seeking to go his way and do his will? While it is of course a very precious, uplifting and devotional time, something that is at the centre of our week and our whole way of living, a witness to our faith, it is also a very solemn service to be at, and, by receiving both bread and wine, to participate in.

The old Book of Common Prayer, in the exhortations in the Communion service that are almost never read let alone used these days, stresses the seriousness of receiving the Communion. Looking at the situation in this generation, with a large number of nominal Christians, many treating going to church and to the Communion (the most usual form of Sunday morning service in many churches) as something to do when it suits our plans, when nothing else is coming in the way such as a day out or family visit, it does make one wonder whether the serious aspects of the covenant meal are being given any thought at all. The Methodist Church, with its annual covenant service held at the beginning of the year, is trying to address this need for commitment (and that service is centred round a Communion service) has appointed that way to deal with this. But surely we want more than an annual reminder of our covenant relationship with God? From the point of view of leading worship, it can well be asked whether our generation of clergy (of all denominations) are giving sufficient thought to this aspect in their leading and preaching, but from the 'place in the pew' we can perhaps be in a better position to make this the subject of our own thoughts and prayers as we prepare and go to the service – in the moments before the service starts, and during the times when there is quiet in the service, so that, if not every time, at least with a degree of regularity, we make ourselves face up to the covenant which we have entered upon when we committed ourselves to being Christ's followers and accepted for ourselves the benefits that come from his giving of himself. There is great value, especially when attending Communion services regularly, in having several themes for meditation and prayer, using one each time (if the sermon in the service does not bring something else to the forefront of our thoughts and silent prayer).

"This is my blood of the new covenant..." said Jesus in the Upper Room on that most sacred of nights. It was to be a new covenant for the Jewish people, but it was also to be far more, for he prayed later that evening "... for those also who will believe in me through their message" (John 17:20). He wanted believers, disciples from all nations, to be brought into the new covenant and to live lives committed to him. That is where we come in.

It is also, we need to remember, a corporate act. We don't celebrate the Communion on our own, we do it together (as that name implies, our Communion being with each other as well as with the Lord). The commitment is something that is shared, and through being shared is strengthened by the act of being together. How much easier it is to keep up a commitment when there is the matter of being helped by others, or of letting others down if we fail to do so. So we are there for each other as we renew our commitment.

What, then, does God want from us through giving us the Communion, instituted during and coming out of the great meal of belonging and commitment that was the Passover? How, we may well ask, does he see the weekly service we attend, and what does he see going through the minds of those gathered there? Does he see those who are thinking of what they are going to get out of the service for themselves, perhaps comfort or support, enjoying the security of the faith, friendship with like-minded people? Does he even see those who are there because of habit, but whose minds are far more on other things? Or does he see a band of people who are the church, meeting together and with him to be strengthened for going out into a new week (day, month) to live out that commitment in everyday life, and knowing that they are strengthened by his presence with them?

But we must move on, for God plan for that evening did not end when the Lord led his followers out of the Upper Room before they had even finished the Passover meal.

10

COMPLETING HIS TASK
See John 14:31b – 15:4; 18:1

Our last chapter ended with Jesus in the Upper Room on the last night of his earthly life. He had been the leader in what he clearly saw as their Passover celebration, with the Twelve as his 'family'; Judas had gone to betray Jesus to the authorities; Jesus has instituted the Holy Communion (as we most usually call it) to be a perpetual memorial of himself, and with much more meaning than that.

What happened next? We have already noticed that Matthew's Gospel tells us that when they had sung a hymn, they went out to the Mount of Olives. It is left to John, as we look carefully at the end of chapter 13, the end of chapter 14, and then again in the first verses of both chapters 17 and 18, to fill in the picture. Clearly, Judas had gone off with a message for the Jewish authorities something like: I know where he is, having a Passover meal in a private house not far from here; it will take perhaps an hour or so before the meal is finished so there is plenty of time for you to go and arrest him. It is not our purpose here to try to work out the motives that led Judas to this act of betrayal. Many have sought to do that, though few have come up with a satisfactory answer.

What would have been clear to Jesus, however, is that if he wanted to do other things that evening it would not be safe to stay in the Upper Room because Judas would be back before long, having been given a detachment of the Temple

Guard (it does not seem as though the Roman soldiers were involved until Jesus was sent to Pilate for judgement). But Jesus needed to complete two very important tasks to finish his ministry before he was arrested, as he knew well that that would be followed by the Cross. One of those tasks was to give the disciples some vital teaching that he had to leave until the very end of his ministry, and the other was to have a final 'report back' – almost de-briefing – prayer time with his Father.

We can't be sure from John's Gospel at what stage the institution of the Holy Communion fitted into the account in John 13 and the teaching in chapter 14. It is natural to surmise that the teaching in chapter 14 came both after Judas had left and the institution of the second part (the cup) of the Communion. We will make that assumption here with the proviso that it might not be the right order. However it hardly matters, for we are looking at the whole evening to see what messages the Father had planned for Jesus to get across, and from which we can learn today.

Notice first that when Jesus told the disciples (John 14:31), "Come now; let us leave", the Passover meal, or rather the full ritual for the evening which did not end when the actual meal had been eaten, was not over. In particular, they had not had the final 'cup' and they had not had the declaration that the annual reminder of the Passover, the celebration of their redemption as a nation, was 'finished' for another year. It would indeed have been very strange for the evening to end without that – as Judas would have known only too well.

So we can imagine that Judas would have returned with the contingent of the guard, only to find that Jesus and the other eleven disciples were not there. Perhaps we can imagine words being spoken and Judas finding himself in a none-too-comfortable situation.

Already though, before they had left it would seem that

Jesus had given the wonderful teaching that we find in chapter 14. We may well wonder why he had left it so much to the last minute, giving that teaching when the disciples were clearly far from relaxed as they sensed that something was about to happen, even if they still did not grasp just what it was – and that despite all the times that we have been told about, starting soon after the Transfiguration, and we can well imagine there would have been others, when Jesus had spoken about what was to happen to him at Jerusalem.

There is a well known principle that you cannot really teach people who are not willing to learn. The disciples, together with many in the nation as we have seen earlier, were looking for their Messiah to come as a national leader. They had not been able to grasp all the implications of what Jesus had been teaching them.

So it was only at this point, when they would have realised that his life was in danger and they were likely to be left without him, that he was able to give very direct teaching on the thought of a place in heaven for his own followers, and the idea that he would come again. It would be at that point in the future therefore (a future which the early church always envisaged as being quite short and in their lifetime) that the concept of his being the sort of King they had envisaged would come to pass.

The other great theme that could only come at this point was the teaching about the Holy Spirit. We had occasion much earlier on (in relation to the coming of the Spirit upon Jesus at his baptism) to comment on the revelation of the Holy Trinity. Although we see that the Holy Spirit was at work in the Incarnation, explicitly in the birth narratives, and in the earthly ministry of Jesus (we are told that he was led by the Spirit), the outpouring and in-filling of believers by the Spirit would come later, as Jesus foretold, and this happened from the day of Pentecost. The great truth of the unity of God was at the very core of Jewish understanding of God. So we don't hear of the Holy Spirit working in or filling the lives of disciples during the period while the Jesus the Son of God, the second person of the Trinity, was present on earth.

Now, as he was preparing to go away, Jesus spoke clearly about how the Spirit is soon to come upon and fill the lives of his followers so that they will be empowered to continue to do his work. Because the Spirit was coming, they would not be alone. In fact Jesus tells them that it was he himself who was going to come to them, albeit in another way. It would be the Spirit who would continue to teach them, to guide them, and thus through them continue the work that Jesus had begun. He so stressed that message that we find it in parts of all three of the chapters which we call the 'last discourse' – John 14, 15 and 16.

That brings us to a question which we will want to answer, and about which the Bible is silent, about which however there are a few clues, and what follows is a possible (putting it no stronger than that) answer to the question.

Chapter 14 seems to have been teaching given when still in the Upper Room, but in a situation of the tension having increased after what must have seemed to the others the very strange situation of Judas being told by Jesus to go and get on with his task. Some thought that he was going to buy provisions as he had been the group's 'treasurer', carrying their money bag; but they had heard the words speaking of betrayal. However, clearly Jesus felt that they were ready for the teaching he gave in John 14.

But then where did they go? Where was the rest of the teaching given? Could it be that Jesus led them to the Temple courts? For most people it was the night before the Passover (remember that Jesus seems to have celebrated it a day earlier than most people), so there would have been large crowds in there. Probably there would have been some sort of illumination by braziers to enable the worshippers to see what they were doing. Could it be that there were some of the teachers of the Law there too, with groups gathered round them? One thing that we know was that the leaders of the Jews did not want to arrest Jesus in a way that would cause uproar in Jerusalem, which would in its turn be a reason for the Roman garrison to intervene and might lead to dire consequences for the Jews' religious freedom. So what happened much later in Gethsemane at the end of that evening, with the arrest taking place long after many of the pilgrims would have gone to their encampments outside the city, and the people in the city being mostly the more compliant regular residents, would have suited them well.

If Jesus had gone to the Temple he would have been able to mingle (together with his group of disciples) in the crowd. In that setting he would have been able to give his teaching, probably sitting down – rather than our having to imagine those chapters being spoken to quite a large group of men walking along in a fairly crowded area. That they were not spoken in Gethsemane is clear from 18:1. It was only after the three previous chapters that they crossed the Kidron Valley, the little river running to the east of Jerusalem, and walked slightly up the lower part of the Mount of Olives to the garden.

Fitting in with this, we find first that the teaching in John 15 is based on the image of the vine. That had links back into the Old Testament, such passages as Jeremiah 2:21 and 6:9, Hosea 10:1 and Joel 2:22, where Israel was spoken of as a vine on more than one occasion. Jesus is now enlarging on that theme and applying it to himself. What we can note is that while we are not aware of vines in the garden of Gethsemane, for it seems to have been an olive orchard or garden rather than a vineyard, we know that the image of the vine had been used a great deal in the carving on the Temple buildings. That was of course linking to what we have just been thinking about concerning Israel, but it could well have been the starting point for the wonderful messages that we find contained in the allegory of the vine which forms so large a part of chapter 15.

The other clue is in 17:1. It was in the place where he had just been talking (so it appears) that Jesus 'looked towards heaven and prayed'. This was a normal posture of the Jews for praying. They looked in the direction they thought of as being God's dwelling place, they usually stood to pray and often they would lift up their hands as they prayed (as some people do today). What would be a more natural place for Jesus to do this than in his Father's house, the Temple? It was where he had worshipped ever since that time when he went there at the age of twelve and had spoken of it then as being his Father's house. While there would have been other people around, probably some of them would have been praying too, so it would not have caused a lot of attention.

In this prayer we find the one example that we have of a fairly long prayer of Jesus. We also have in this prayer what seems to be akin to Jesus reporting to his Father that the tasks that he had been given to do during his ministry had been completed: "I have brought you glory on earth by completing the work you gave me to do" (John 17:6).

Then he went on to pray for the eleven whom he was leaving behind, and his other followers, and also, in what we often see as the third section of the prayer, praying for the church, which would follow down through the centuries, even if that duration was not clear at that time. It is in this lovely, precious prayer which we often call his 'high priestly prayer' that Jesus prays for, pleads for, his followers to remain united.

What a message that is for us. It is the final time during

his life that he was free to speak and teach, and it was then that he gave the call for unity. We are only too well aware of how the church (worldwide as well as down through the centuries) has in many ways failed to fulfil that, though there is indeed a special awareness of unity in the Spirit between true believers which has nothing to do with institutional ecclesiastical structures.

There is no other place in Scripture where Jesus speaks so clearly (and we might say passionately) about the unity of disciples.

So we come to ask ourselves the question that we have come back to so many times already: why did God want these chapters to be included in the account of Jesus' life that has been passed down to us? The three synoptic Gospels say nothing about what happened between instituting the Communion and Gethsemane. Yet the chapters of the Final Discourse in John's Gospel are for many some of the most precious ones in the Bible, and give amazing teaching. They are a very clear report of what he said. Again we think of how astonishing it was that he was able to give that teaching at such a time! Without that instruction, despite all that is given in the other parts of the New Testament under the guidance of the Holy Spirit, we would be very much poorer. Surely this passage must rank among the special aspects that the Father had planned for the life of his Son.

But we go forward. I can almost imagine Jesus leaving with that small band of frightened and bewildered disciples, not by the vast main entrance to the Temple with its imposing steps on the south side, but by the doorway on the north side, proceeding from there to one of the city gates and on down the slope to the Kidron Valley. Gethsemane was only slightly up from the valley bottom, on the road which he would have known so well as it led up and over the top of the Mount of Olives and to Bethany. It was also the main road to Jericho, the route which so many pilgrims took to go to Jerusalem and the route that he had followed on Palm Sunday morning. It seems very likely that Jesus had been given permission by its owner to use that Garden of Gethsemane and that he had been there a good few times, for how else would Judas have known to look there for Jesus? With every bit of space round Jerusalem being used for camping over the festival, to have such a retreat that was private would have been a great resource for Jesus. Perhaps it leads to the devotional question that we can ask ourselves as to how willing we are for Jesus to use for his purposes the things we own, whether our homes, our gardens or much smaller things? In particular, can our Christian homes be havens of peace to which people can come to find the refreshment and spiritual help that they need?

But of course for us, indeed for all Christians, the name of the Garden of Gethsemane immediately brings to our thoughts the agony of Jesus and his prayer as he awaited the arrival of Judas, whom he knew would soon be coming.

Some of us know what it is to wait for something very unpleasant, perhaps a serious operation or a very difficult interview. It is the waiting and wondering what it will be like and whether we can cope that is often worse than dealing with the actual situation itself when the time comes. We can deal with the pain when it happens, with the restrictions and being told what to do and the things that are said, it is the anticipation that we find so difficult. So it must have been with Jesus, but there was another aspect for him which we can never fully comprehend.

He was the sinless Son of God, who had right through his life and ministry on earth had the closest contact and relationship with his Father, a relationship totally unclouded (as opposite to the way that ours must always be) by the barriers caused by sin. To carry the guilt of the sin of the whole world and for all generations, as he was to do on the Cross, would have been a tremendous burden and something we cannot even begin to comprehend.

In the Old Testament, one who offered a sacrifice would lay his hand on the head of the animal as a symbol of the transfer of guilt from himself to the victim, before the victim was slain. All we know is that when Jesus went to the Cross he carried that load – that barrier between God and man – of sin. Whether he already felt the load on him in the Garden is not really important, for the anticipation was there. It has often been remarked that many men have faced death with great bravery but they were not bearing the burden of all the sin of other people, nor the thought of separation from God, while it was all happening. Yet this was the experience that Jesus had to face in the Garden, and we can see why it was that the Father allowed it to happen. So many have found that it is in seeking to come alongside Jesus (in our thoughts) as he agonised and waited in the Garden, that we can understand better the awfulness and burden of sin.

It was in that time – and we cannot know how long a time it was, whether only perhaps half an hour or much longer, the length does not matter for under that situation every minute must have seemed like an hour – that the two natures of the person of Jesus, the divine and the human, are seen together: the divine, with the determination to do the Father's will and the knowledge that he could at any moment stop going through it by calling on heavenly resources; the human with the agony of anticipation and the knowledge of betrayal by one who had been in his band of close friends, made worse by those who were with him now sleeping, worn out by all that had been happening, the stress of the past days and the sense of coming trouble, and the experiences of that evening. By this time it must have been around midnight.

We need to do all we can to understand what Jesus went

through on that evening. Like nothing else, it enables us to understand the wonder of the love of God for us, in that the Father allowed and the Son endured (without being forced to do so by the Father but of his own free will) such agony. From our 'chrysalis' viewpoint, seeking to stand back a little and see the wonder of the overall plan of God, we can thank Jesus for going through this, for the sin of the world and for each one of us. We can each say "he did it for me" personally. We thank God for letting us have the record of all that happened on that sacred evening.

11

THE CROSS

See John 19:28–30

As we come to this point, and start looking at the events of
the few hours that culminated in the Cross of Jesus, we need
perhaps to go back for a moment to see where we have come.
It is not our purpose here to think in a deeply devotional
way about the physical suffering of Jesus, during his trials
and then on the Cross itself, important though that is for all
Christians; our purpose throughout this study has been to
ask the question as to why in the life of Jesus (and that of
course includes the account of his suffering and death) it was
the Father's plan for the various events within the narrative
to take place. We are trying to see more of the divine view
(if we can say that with great reverence) and why particular
key events took place within God's purposes as we take an
overview, looking at the amazing plan of redemption for the
world that involved the sending of God's only-begotten Son
into the world to save sinners.

God's plan had to involve the Incarnation, when the Son
of God took the nature of a man, entering the world as any
other person would, through birth from his human mother
and thus sharing in humanity as a baby, as a small child,
and through the years of growth and development. It was
a path that meant Jesus had to experience ordinary life as
a Jewish boy of that era, following the path of Judaistic

practice, sharing in the ceremony of *Bar Mitzvah*, living an ordinary life in a small town, later working to earn his living as a carpenter.

But it was also the path that led on to ministry, and we have seen how that started by once again sharing with ordinary people, this time as they responded to the preaching of the great forerunner John the Baptist, a response that meant re-dedicating themselves to being God's people through the ritual cleansing of baptism.

From this point there were what seem like two separate themes in Jesus' earthly ministry. We have been following the thought of his preaching the message of the kingdom of God and of his showing forth by example the love of God for individuals. We have also begun to see what is meant by living as one of his followers, as members of the kingdom, as people who have responded to the call and accepted what we came to see in chapter nine was involved by living under the new covenant relationship with God.

Yet at the same time, ever since the Transfiguration story, we have realised that the path that Jesus was treading was increasingly centred upon being a journey to the Cross. It is the final part of that path that we need to look at now. Of course there is the need to be deeply sensitive to, as well as immensely grateful for, all the suffering that Jesus endured as a man in going along that path – in the betrayal, in the trials before the High Priest and Pilate, in the mocking, in the walk to the Cross, and while he suffered upon the Cross. That suffering must never be played down. It was suffering that was totally undeserved, because he was sinless. It was made infinitely worse for him by bearing the load of the world's sin, and with it a barrier coming between himself and the Father as shown by his words on the Cross: "My God, my God, why have you forsaken me?" (Mark 15:34).

But we remember that our purpose is very specific: to try

to understand how it was that the Father, right through the life of Jesus (and of course that includes these final hours), allowed or ordained that certain things happened in order to bring messages to our human race. The aspects that we have been considering have all been attempting to show this. The wonder is that Jesus, even through all his suffering, the physical pain and the mental and spiritual stress, was able to think not only about the suffering of those around him, as witnessed by his provision for Mary his mother, but also in carrying out by his words and actions the details that carried the messages upon which we can dwell as we seek to understand the astounding way the suffering that Jesus endured is linked to what had been foretold by word or events right back through the Old Testament. After the resurrection, Jesus spoke to the two disciples whom he met on the Emmaus road about what had happened and what was written in the Old Testament: 'And beginning with Moses and all the Prophets, he explained to them what was said in all the Scriptures concerning himself' (Luke 24:27, NIV). How we would love to have a verbatim account of what he said let alone been a 'fly on the wall' as he spoke! All we can do is to try to look in the Old Testament to get the clues, as well as passages elsewhere in the New Testament that show what the early Christians were seeing as the answers to this.

So we turn to what happened after the arrest of Jesus. We are told he was taken to the High Priest's residence. Only comparatively recently an alternative suggestion has come to be put forward that suggests a different location of this, a site not far from where the Jaffa Gate to the old city now stands, but we need not worry at this point about the location as our main concern is the event itself.

The trial before the Jewish authorities, who were the religious leaders allowed under the Roman rulers to have a large measure of independence in running the affairs of

Jewish ordinary life and yet with a religious overtone behind the way in which they did this, was concerned primarily with a charge of blasphemy, but the real issue in their minds was that this (to them) unqualified teacher was going so to stir things up among the population as to lead to unrest, so that their semi-independence would be compromised with the Romans and their authority undermined within the Jewish nation. Blasphemy, which they thought to be what was happening when Jesus spoke of his relationship with the Father, was the charge upon which they hung their case – which was never looked at, because they had prejudged it weeks if not months before, without Jesus being present and able to answer for himself. Everything depended on their understanding of the books of the Law, the Old Testament Torah, and allowed no place for what we have just spoken of when thinking of what Jesus said to those on the Emmaus road. Condemnation was therefore a foregone conclusion. Yet, in what they did, they were acting as the representatives of the Jewish people in the rejection of their Messiah. We can look, though not without some sympathy for them in how they saw things, at Isaiah 53:3, 'He was despised and rejected by men'. How all this ties in with what had happened a few days earlier as Jesus entered Jerusalem on Palm Sunday, seeing the city and weeping over it, with the words, "If you, even you, had only known on this day what would bring you peace..." (see Luke 19:42, NIV).

So with Jesus having been condemned to death for a Jewish 'crime' (and we can look at John 11:50 to see how the High Priest spoke of it as being better for one man to die than the whole nation perish), the Jewish leaders were faced with a dilemma. The difficulty was that such a charge would not carry any weight with the Romans, yet to put Jesus to death on their own (as was done later with Stephen) would have been extremely unwise, if not illegal. Hence there was the need for them to take Jesus before Pilate and there present their case, charging him with a crime that the Romans would accept without question as being worthy of the death penalty. On top of that we note that the Jewish leaders did not want to go into the Governor's palace on the eve of the Passover as that would have made them ceremonially unclean (this gives a clear indication as to what day this was happening on). Pilate understood, and he tried the case outside and so in public.

The whole story of the trial before Pilate is very well-known, but for our purposes there are two things that we need to focus on. The first is that Pilate questioned Jesus about the charge that they were bringing: namely that he was claiming to be a king and therefore on the face of it guilty of a treasonable act against Caesar, something that Pilate could not ignore. It was here that Jesus made the clearest claim to being a king that we find anywhere in the Gospels. He spoke too of having a kingdom that was 'not of this world' (John 18:36), and so his servants would not fight. We can see more of the nature of his kingship when we read the Book of Revelation. He is heaven's king, and the full glory of that kingship is his.

What a tremendous concept this brings to us. Here is Jesus, the Son of God, declaring his divine position, and doing it when brought as a condemned criminal (by the Jews) before Caesar's representative. How easy it is for us, as we read and re-read the narrative, to concentrate upon all that Jesus was suffering, and fail to notice that in the midst of not only suffering but humiliation and rejection he is making the greatest claim about his nature. It was a claim that put Pilate in a dilemma himself, for he did not know how to respond.

The second point for us to make is that what was to happen in this trial, not once but several times as recorded by the evangelists Luke (23:4, 14) and John (18:38; 19:4, 6), Pilate declares that he does not find Jesus guilty.

When we look at the way that the Old Testament speaks of the presenting of lambs for sacrifice, time and again we see that the lamb has to be 'without blemish', which means that it has to be outwardly perfect and in no way deformed or mutilated. If it was to be a substitute for an imperfect person, a sinner, it had to be perfect so that the guilt of the person could be transferred to the animal, making that the imperfect one and the person who was offering the sacrifice guiltless. It is a theme that comes many times in the Old Testament, for instance in Leviticus 22:17–25 and in Deuteronomy 15:21; 17:1. We also see a telling passage in Malachi 1:6–8, speaking of how people would not dare to bring an imperfect animal to the temple as their offering, implying that the priests were those who gave the animal an examination to make sure that it was 'without blemish' and fit to be an offering. Here then is Jesus, who was declared right at the start of his ministry by John the Baptist as being 'the Lamb of God, who takes away the sin of the world' (see John 1:29, cp. v. 36) being now declared by the highest judge in the land, the representative of the Roman Emperor, as being without any guilt – and that not just once but, as we have seen, several times.

Let us just think for a moment about the time when this was happening. We have just seen that it was the day of preparation of the Passover, that is the day before the vast majority of the people would be holding their Passover meal (their new day started at sunset, so the day before was what we would call earlier the same day), and by this time it would be well into the morning. One account speaks of the trial ending about the 'sixth hour', so round about noon, while elsewhere we gather that Jesus was on the Cross (because of the period when an unnatural darkness came over the land) from the sixth until the ninth hour. It would have been during that morning that many men (and only men) would have been bringing their family's Passover lamb to the priests in the Temple, to be slaughtered in readiness for the Passover meal that they would all be observing that evening.

Does it all tie up with our Christian message and understanding? Jesus, whom Paul spoke of in 1 Corinthians 5:7 as being 'our Passover lamb' who has been sacrificed for us, was being cleared (if we may use that term) by the highest judge in the land, the Governor himself, as being without blemish – therefore able to be a sacrifice. Then he was taken to the place of sacrifice at the very time when the ritual of lambs being slaughtered was happening only a very short distance way and in the same city. We don't know for certain whether the trial of Jesus was in the fortress which was the Roman garrison's headquarters and directly to the north of the Temple (a place where many visiting pilgrims today are taken) or elsewhere in Pilate's residence. That does not really matter. What does matter is that the place of crucifixion was on Mount Moriah, the very mountain where God's 'dress rehearsal' took place when Abraham was told to offer his son Isaac as a sacrifice and then substituted at the last moment for a lamb (see Genesis 22:2ff), and of course the site upon which many centuries later the Temple was built in the time of King Solomon.

It all helps us to realise that both the place and the timing of the crucifixion of Jesus were so perfectly arranged by God, and why Jesus again and again spoke of 'my time', the time for him to go to the Cross.

It is not our purpose to look in detail at the actual suffering of Jesus upon the Cross, even though we must never allow ourselves to take it all for granted simply because we have read and heard the account so many times in our lives. Nor are we going to look here at some of the most wonderful moments in those hours, or at the 'seven words', the seven times that are recorded when Jesus spoke while on the Cross.

We can note, though, one very amazing thing before we move on to the moments of the crucifixion narrative. Jesus on the cross was not just thinking about himself and the terrible pain that he was being forced to endure, nor dwelling on the utter humiliation that he was facing as Son of God, in being executed in this fashion, nor even the load of guilt which had been laid on him. In the midst of it all, he thought about his grief-stricken mother and made provision for her. That he was able to do this speaks to us not only of the wonder of his compassion, but also illustrates that in some amazing way he was able to give attention to the details of what was happening, not just around him but actually in what he was doing. Surely the words that he spoke from the cross were not things that, as we would say, 'came into his head' as he suffered, they were words again that fit in closely with the theme that we have been following all through these chapters.

You will remember that we spoke earlier of when Jesus came to the closing of the Passover in the Upper Room (and it had been only about twelve or fifteen hours earlier). He had had the meal, spoke to the eleven disciples who were still there with the teaching recorded for us in John 14, and then abruptly left the Upper Room because (as we assumed, looking at the practical side and the events that were happening) Judas would soon return with the party of guards to arrest him. But perhaps there was much more lying behind the fact of Jesus (apparently) finishing the Passover meal early. Let us explore the idea, for it is only an idea and certainly not something that we can be sure about, and so people will have different views.

We made the point that, when he left, the Passover celebration was not finished even though all the main parts of the evening's traditional ritual had taken place. The Passover still had certain things that had to happen even though the whole evening is usually conducted in an informal fashion. In particular there were two final things that had to take place before the full ritual of the Passover evening could to be said to have ended. Remember we made the point that Jesus clearly intended the events of that evening to be the Passover meal for himself and his disciples even though it was probably a day early (perhaps on a day that a minority of Jews were observing). Surely he would not fail to complete it on that occasion of all occasions?

Maybe we can find an answer, and in so doing marvel more than ever about the wonder of God's planning and timing which we have been thinking about right the way through, as we look at the events that took place at the Cross itself.

Jesus went to the Cross, as our Passover, bearing the sins of the world. Peter speaks of how he was without sin and then bore our sins (1 Peter 2:22, 24); we have seen that he was not just observing the Passover but actually was our Passover.

When Jesus was being nailed to the cross he was offered a drink of wine mixed with myrrh (Mark 15:23), a form of painkiller apparently often given by sympathetic bystanders to those about to be crucified, but he refused it, presumably because he wanted to bear the full cost of salvation. But when we come towards the end of the period on the Cross, about the 'ninth hour' so about three o'clock in the afternoon, Jesus said "I am thirsty" (John 19:28), and he was given a drink, offered by a sponge on a stick. Could this possibly have been in his mind the 'missing' final cup of the Passover, which is thought of as the cup marking the completion of the Passover, except for one final declaration? Could this have been in his mind when he spoke in the Garden of desiring that "this cup" was one he would not have to drink?

In the meal, when all have drunk from that final cup, the

leader declares the end of the evening's ceremonial and celebration with declaring that it is 'finished'.

How amazing that Jesus did the same thing! John 19:30 tells of him saying "It is finished." Perhaps we can put those words before the statement given as his final words in Luke 23:46, "Father, into your hands I commit my spirit." If we are correct in this, we have the final two pieces of the Passover (spoken you remember by the one who *is* our Passover) taking place on the Cross itself before he committed himself to the Father, 'bowed his head and gave up his spirit' (John 19:30).

Surely even to contemplate this fills us with wonder at the way in which the whole sequence of events – from the start of the meal to the end of the time on the Cross – works out. Once again we are amazed that Jesus could be in such control of himself at that point, despite the terrible suffering he was enduring, and nothing must allow us to be so thinking of the theory of all this that we fail to give full prominence to that suffering, right to the point of death.

But we need to take this farther, for it makes us see again the meaning of the crucifixion as being, in the eyes of God, very much linked to the meaning of the Passover. The latter is a reminder of the rescue or redemption of Israel from Egypt, the cost of that event, and how it meant the setting free of the people whom God had chosen. So we are brought to see that, in the eyes of God, the death of Jesus is also linked very closely to the message of redemption, and this time a far greater redemption of the whole world through the propitiatory offering of God's Son. Whether modern thought likes it or not, whether this idea is congenial to the ears of people in the twenty-first century and in the West, we cannot escape making the link.

All through these pages, our aim is to see the events in the life of Jesus in a way that tries to look at the way in which

God planned. To take this view of the crucifixion is in no way to denigrate the place and importance of many other messages, attitudes and viewpoints. Of course the Cross is the most wonderful demonstration of the love of God in action, with Jesus' total self-giving. Of course we see the result of awful injustice on the part of the Jewish and Roman authorities, with a prejudicial presumption of guilt based on the desires of those very priests and leaders who thought their way of serving God was the only one, and that their position, and that of the Temple, was to be maintained at all costs. Of course we have in Jesus the wonderful example for us to follow in putting the service of others before ourselves, even in the face of extreme danger. Of course we see in him the example, leading us to take up our cross and follow him (see Matthew 16:24), knowing that the right path in life is not always the easy one. None of these messages, nor all the devotional thoughts and actions that come from them, is to be forgotten.

But we are brought back again and again to the plan of God – through the observance of the command to Israel to keep the annual celebration of the Passover and redemption from Egypt some fifteen hundred years earlier. We see this in the setting for the death of Jesus – something so clearly planned, regardless of the anguish of facing it, by his deliberately organising his journey to Jerusalem for his 'hour' to be linked to that Passover – the interpretation that he wanted to dominate our understanding.

How can we close this part of our study but by looking back yet again in our minds at the whole plan as we have come to see it (perhaps reminding ourselves by re-reading the chapter headings) and coming before our wonderful God with a deep sense of wonder, worship and thankfulness for what he has done, for the obedience of Jesus (see Philippians 2:6–8) and for the redemption of the world and of us personally. At the same time we renew our allegiance to him under the new covenant sealed with his blood.

12

RESURRECTION
See 1 Corinthians 15:51 and 1 John 3:2

How easy it is to think of the final words of Jesus on the Cross, "It is finished", and see that as though it was the end of his work on earth, for he had done what was necessary for our redemption, so that the consequences of God's righteousness meeting sin, and thus sinful people, are 'redeemed' by what he has done through being our Passover sacrificed for us (see again 1 Corinthians 5:7). For us, living a long time after, it is as though the debt, the penalty for sin that our just God would have to apply to us, has been paid for us already, and is there for us to receive through our redemption (his work) and our faith (responding to it); it is all an act of his grace. Thus we may be tempted to think that what follows cannot be so important.

Often, gospel sermons end with an appeal to accept what Jesus did on the Cross as being for you, with no mention of his resurrection and how Jesus is Lord. Yet we have the triumphant Easter story, the message that comes with it, and then the Ascension of Jesus. Most traditional churches teach that Easter is the most important festival in the Christian calendar, and that has been the view held in churches since Christianity became the established religion of the Roman empire. But for so many we meet today, people who are very willing to accept the Easter holiday, whether following the end of a school or college term or as a long weekend break from the usual routine of work, there is little thought of the Christian festival. Many people today don't know what Easter is about and don't care.

Christians are often spoken of as 'Easter people', for we are living in the light of the message that Jesus rose from the dead, and he is still our risen, living Lord. But while the meaning of the resurrection is of the greatest importance for every Christian, for none is it more so than those in the 'chrysalis' stage of life. Those of us who have reached that strange period in our lives and realise that there is little time left for us here on earth, after what is after all a very short period when seen in the light of history let alone the time that life has been on earth, are in no doubt at all, if we hold the Christian faith, that this is the message above all others that we are clinging to.

Where would we be without Easter? Many of us have been taught the message ever since we were small children, whether at home, in church or even in school (the latter less likely now than used to be the case). But at the same time we have to accept that for many people in our churches it is not the easiest message for them to be able to explain to others who are outside the faith, nor really to grasp the full implications of it for themselves. We know what happened and we may also be aware that some Christians find it hard to understand all the individual events recorded in the four Gospels. Various explanations of the chronology have been proposed. One such appeared in the book 'Easter Enigma' by John Wenham (1984), but nobody would want to say that this is definitely the answer. Much more recently, a fascinating chronological account of Holy Week and the events of the Passion, the death and burial of Jesus has been proposed by David Pawson in his book *Jesus: The Seven Wonders of History* (2013, Anchor). He points to the significance of the mention in John 19:31 of a special or "high" Sabbath (with which the Passover began, and which could be on any day of the week) and the difference between the Roman and Jewish calendars. Once again we find that what some have mistakenly seen as a discrepancy can in fact be harmonised perfectly when the historical context is known and understood.

However, it is not our purpose here to try to piece all the individual aspects together, rather we are seeking in our studies to take the basic fact of Jesus rising from the dead, of how he is still the risen, living Lord, and relating that to the faith of a Christian in the 'chrysalis' stage of life. If it has a special resonance at that stage, it is vital for Christians of *all* ages to see this as being the central truth of the gospel message that we hold dear. How right Paul was when he wrote, 'If only for this life we have hope in Christ, we are to be pitied more than all men' (1 Corinthians 15:19, *NIV*).

As we come near to the end of our lives, some of us feel as though we are approaching a shut door. We sense that there is something on the other side, and know that the door can open to let people through; we have confidence that it will do so for us, but the very uncertainty of what lies beyond makes us uneasy, to say the least. It is not just the fact of stepping out of this life, a life which is all we have known, that makes us uneasy, but also a sense of uncertainty about the form of life, something beyond our real comprehension now, which lies beyond, as well as the thought of coping with any disability that may go with a final illness and approaching death. But even in that, the message of the death and resurrection of Jesus rings out with the knowledge that he who went through extremes of pain on the Cross is right here with us, through his Holy Spirit. Perhaps you have already had a serious illness – if so, then you will know how important, how real, was the sense of the presence of Jesus with you then, even if you did not feel able to talk to him (perhaps not even silently) in long or well-constructed prayers. Just being aware of him, and being able to lean on him, was enough.

However there should not be fear of death. We do know a great deal about what lies beyond that 'door', for not only have we (who have come to know and walk with Jesus) met and are now living with the one who has been through that door and has come back, but we find in the accounts of his Passion, death and resurrection so much to help us. The same Lord whom we know and trust in our everyday lives, and to whom we talk each day in prayer, is the one who died and rose again and is now there in heaven awaiting us. 'We shall see him as he is' (see 1 John 3:2).

We are not going to look in detail at the accounts of the empty tomb and the resurrection here, but rather we will pick up on some of the messages and implications of what we can call another 'three Rs'.

The first is that *Jesus is risen*. That simple statement is both about what happened at the moment when he rose from the dead and also the present situation: that Jesus is still the living one who has been through the 'door' that we have been speaking about. The power of death has been broken so that it is not now an end, but for the Christian a stage on the journey. So we tend to say 'He is risen' rather than 'He rose', though of course both are true.

In ways that we cannot fully comprehend, sin and death's power are closely linked in Scripture. How the Fall of man, recorded in Genesis, affects the physical death of people down through the centuries and even today, we may find it hard to understand, but we accept that, as sin put a barrier between God and man, so death is the symbol of that. As most people look at death they see it simply as an end, either the end of everything for their lives, or the end of what they understand. Many have a feeling that there is something beyond death, and in the post-Christian culture we are in for many there is the thought of God being involved but the lack of a relationship with him makes it all very vague. Many people try a 'pick and choose' approach to religious belief to formulate their own ideas out of the teaching of different religions, and that gets reflected in their thinking about death and what follows it. Death is often thought to be the end of everything, but Jesus was raised from death to life, breaking the power of death for all who live 'in him'.

"In him was life" (John 1:4). Jesus has eternal life in himself and is the source of eternal life for those who believe and trust in him. When we have that relationship with him, we can claim, in the words of John, that: 'God has given us eternal life, and this life is in his Son. He who has the Son has life' (See 1 John 5:11–12). This is a truth for the present, not only the future. We can be *in* Jesus Christ *now* in this present life. As Paul put it in 2 Timothy 1:12, '... I know whom I have believed, and am convinced that he is able to guard what I have entrusted to him for that day.' (NIV)

We are trusting in the fact that 'He himself bore our sins in his body on the tree....' (See 1 Peter 2:24, NIV.) We believe that was sufficient to close the gulf between us and God. The eternal life we have begun to know in Christ will continue in the world to come. We can know that Jesus has shown that death is not the end, and he has opened the way for us.

This was the basis of the faith of the first Christians, and when we come to know Jesus we have that same sense of expectation. Some reading this may have experienced being very ill and the possibility of death. Whatever the feelings about leaving family, friends and our life here, when we are Christians there is not the feeling of our whole life being extinguished (if we can use that illustration) but of being borne up by Christ as we move forward. What a difference that makes to everything about us when we reach the 'chrysalis' stage of life, and wonder whether we will be around this time next year or next month. Our thoughts are less about the leaving and more on where we are going. It is almost an adventure to look forward to. So there is our first 'R': he is risen. Jesus had to go through all that went before, for us to know this truth and the wonderful assurance it gives us.

Now we come on to the second 'R'. When Jesus was raised from the dead and came to the eleven disciples, and then to others who had the privilege of meeting him, it was clearly shown that he had been raised from death to life. Death had no power to hold him. Now we find that in the succeeding weeks, Jesus *revealed* to his followers many truths. It all started on the evening of the day of resurrection, when Jesus spoke to Cleopas and his companion on the Emmaus road, and told them of how what had happened to him on the cross had been foretold in the Old Testament (see Luke 24:25–27).

We have various accounts in the Gospels about those forty days before the Ascension, and there were other times as well when they met with Jesus. The Gospels don't say much about what Jesus said on the various occasions, but there is a reference in Acts 1:3 which hints at much more: 'He appeared to them over a period of forty days and spoke to them about the kingdom of God.' How we would love to know more about what he said, but then perhaps we do know more about it, for it could well be that much of the understanding that the apostles had, and which formed the basis of their preaching and writing, was based on the things he said to them over that period. It could not have been taught before the cross and resurrection had happened.

It is for this reason that we can be confident that the period when the risen Lord was appearing to them and preparing them for his leaving them to carry on his work after he ascended to heaven (and thus bringing an end to the period of appearing to them sometimes, yet not visible to them all the time) was a period for much teaching. Perhaps it was a time of piecing together the things he had said to them before, which they had not fully understood.

There is another very important aspect of what Jesus revealed at that time: he was able to show them something of the nature of the resurrection body that his followers will one day have, because he had it first.

Paul, in 1 Corinthians 15:20, 23, speaks of Jesus being the 'firstfruits' of those who will rise to a new life. The picture Paul uses here is from the Jewish festivals. They were told to bring to the Temple the first ripe corn, seeing it as a promise that there would be the full harvest following on, and thus to thank God in advance for what was to come. What a lovely idea! Later, they came at the Feast of Tabernacles to have what we would think of as a harvest festival, thanking God for all the harvest which had then been gathered in. So, Paul is teaching, the resurrection body of Jesus was like what we would call today a prototype, showing what the 'production model' will be like, the body that we will have when he comes again in glory. Can we use that similarly as something to thank God for in advance of our having it? On this basis we can again find a wonderful sense of security, even if many aspects of what that body is really like are still what we might call a 'trade secret'. Those first Christians were able to look at it from its visible appearance, so we have that to go on, but Jesus said to Mary (in John 20:17), "Do not hold on to me", or as it is in the AV, "Touch Me not". As with so many things in the Bible about the afterlife, we are told all we need to know and yet realise that we are not in a position as yet to fully understand what will be revealed. Paul tells us: 'I consider that our present sufferings are not worth comparing with the glory that will be revealed in us.

The creation waits in eager expectation for the sons of God to be revealed' (Romans 8:18–19, *NIV*).

But it is time to move on to the third 'R'. The church rightly stresses these days, through the inclusion of the Feast of the Ascension in the Easter period, that the two are inseparably linked. Our third 'R' speaks to us of Jesus restored to his full glory, in his rightful place, his position of *reigning* at the right hand of the Father, when his time on earth was completed.

Let us look briefly at those related aspects, for as we view life in a different way when we come to the 'chrysalis' stage, we need to have them firmly in our minds, and we can be sure that God wants us to have a clear picture of the truths about what lies ahead for us. Things that seemed very distant during our younger years, things that then we treated as more of a theory than something that could imminently change our whole situation, suddenly seem very much the practical issues which we need to face and try to understand for ourselves, especially if we have been told that we have a condition that might well lead to the end of our life here. There have been times historically when death seemed an ever-present issue for everybody, when life expectancy was short, very few families raised all their children, illnesses were much more likely to be fatal – even things which we now treat as comparatively minor. A look at a page in a village burial register of the late nineteenth century showed, on one opening, fourteen entries, half having been burials of children. There are parts of the world where lives are still cut short through disease, famine and high perinatal mortality. But it seems as though in our society people want to treat the end of life as something that is always a long way off and only to be spoken about in a way that disguises the reality with euphemisms. We might say someone 'passed away', 'when something happens' or use similar expressions. It is spoken of as though it is always terrible, yet for the Christian it should be seen as something very different from that. Many people are often well into adulthood before they have to face the funeral of somebody close to them, and then they find it very difficult to cope with. Many are retired before their parents die.

Yet as we get older things seem different. The fact of our own mortality is, if not in the forefront, at least 'in the back of our minds' on a regular basis. We need to be ready, and that means not only having what some call a 'saving faith' in Jesus, and having practical arrangements in place to make it as easy as possible for those we leave behind, but also grasping the truths about how our faith is going to change our whole attitude and gives us an idea about what to expect.

Jesus has gone to get things ready for us; we are told that in John 14:2 by Jesus himself speaking in the Upper Room on that last night before the Cross. He will come again in glory. His whole church should prepare and be ready for him. We know that for those of us who will pass into his presence through the gateway of a normal death (however suddenly or drawn-out the actual time of making the transformation is) he has prepared a place for us. His work in heaven, with all that is involved with reigning – being our Lord and Saviour – is still very much concerned with having all ready to welcome us there when it is the right time.

We have already thought of Jesus having being restored to his full glory. That fact is something to give us confidence. When we look at the Book of Revelation, we see Jesus still as man yet with all his heavenly glory (as well as showing himself as the Lamb who was slain). No longer do we picture him as the man of Galilee who was rejected; we think now with confidence that our beloved Lord is in all his heavenly glory – a glory that is beyond our understanding. But the fact that he still has his manhood makes us realise that he still has the same depth of understanding of our position here.

Sometimes we may feel that we are of little consequence as individuals in the vastness of the world's population, and of the whole of humanity down through the ages, let alone being in a world that is a tiny speck in the vastness of the universe. But then we realise that we have a personal relationship with heaven's King, that we are able to come to him now in prayer (do we grasp the privilege which that is, and show the fact in the way we speak to him?) and we are going to move one day into his presence.

Let us take some words from St. Paul: 'we will all be changed' (see 1 Corinthians 15:51). That is true whether through being here and being transformed at the time when he returns, or through passing into the new life of heaven through death. Or look at 1 John 3:2b, '...we shall be like him, for we shall see him as he is.' (NIV)

When we pass from this life we are passing into the timelessness of eternity. Those who die before Jesus returns in glory are not going to be on a different footing to those who are caught up at that event when he returns for us to be with him as we are taught in 1 Thessalonians 4:17. Whichever way it happens, we go to be with the one who went ahead, having shown himself alive from the dead.

This leads us back again to the Gospel records and the message that God has for us there. In one sense, we look on the resurrection narratives as being the climax to the life of Jesus and to the message of our salvation. Yet there were the forty days when he was seen, not all the time, but suddenly coming amongst his friends and disciples. Perhaps they thought that it would go on like that, but then came the Ascension, for Jesus was taken from them in a visible way into heaven. Clearly, God wanted the message of that day to be seen as something of great importance, as well as linked to the two things which were to follow, namely: the gift of the Holy Spirit at Pentecost and the promise of Jesus' return in glory.

We can see these two things as being God's wonderful provision for us. Life for us, as for the first Christians, goes on – but not on our own. How well it has been said that the Holy Spirit is 'Jesus in another form', able to be wherever Christians are, living not just with them but in them, and enabling them to be the people that God wants us all to be. We can link this back to the teaching ministry of Jesus which we were looking at earlier in this book, but we are not just given our instructions and expected to carry on, for we have him with us to teach, lead and enable us to be what he wants us to be.

And then there is the other aspect of his provision: the promise of the second coming of Jesus. This sets before us the knowledge that life will not just go on and on until the world is in a state when it cannot support its population or a catastrophe occurs. God knows the situation, and at his own time Jesus will come again. We need not worry ourselves about when that will be, so long as we are living in such a way that when he comes he will find us living, and being and speaking, and filling our time, in such a way that will be pleasing to him and under his guidance and plan. Some have called this 'living in the light of the Lord's return' and that is a good phrase to use. We are told again and again in the Old Testament, especially in Deuteronomy, that the people of Israel were to live in a way that obeyed the covenant that God had made with them through all he had done for them. Every time we go to the Holy Communion we are reminded that "This is my blood of the new covenant", so we too are expected to follow the teaching of the Lord who gave us this covenant relationship.

Perhaps this is a good point at which to end our looking at how God is speaking to us through the major events and phases in the life of Jesus. We need to be able to hold it all together, seeing not first one narrative and then another but looking at the whole wonderful account as being a unity. Have you ever tried reading through one of the Gospels in much the same way as you would any other book – not in short readings of a few verses but, if not reading a whole Gospel, at least a fair number of chapters at one time, and trying to read it all over two or three days? While not a substitute for the detailed study of a short passage, it is one of the best ways to get an understanding of the life of Jesus as a whole.

13

PERSPECTIVES
See John 10:10b

It is quite a few years now since men went to the moon. Some can remember all the excitement that went with that first visit, with the thought that men had been able to achieve that. They were able to go to an alien environment, fulfil their purpose there and then return safely to earth. What a wonderful achievement it was. But while they were there they were very restricted, for there was no atmosphere so they had to wear space suits including the means to be able to breathe; they could only move a very short distance; their travel there was in a very cramped situation in a tiny capsule so different from the freedom of movement they enjoyed on earth.

We know, too, that there were many other aspects to their achievement. They were able to carry out experiments and even bring back fragments of moon rock so that they could be analysed. For those who had worked hard to get ready for those other tests, that experiment on which they had expended so much effort must have been the thing that really mattered. They were so very keen for the advancement of knowledge, of science in that particular sphere, that this was the thing that really counted as far as they were concerned, the aspect of the great achievement that met up with their own situation and their work, their need in the advancement of science. For many that would be an endeavour of great practical importance.

Perhaps we can see a parable in all this. There was the main achievement, with Jesus coming to the world, an environment so totally different from his heavenly home. To make a comparison between his life here on earth and in heaven is impossible for us, since we have no experience as yet of what heaven is like. But Jesus came to fulfil the divine purpose in all the aspects we have been considering and many more, and then he returned to his heavenly home.

What we have sought to see, as we have been going through a few of those main aspects and events of Jesus' life and ministry on earth, is something of the purposes of the Father which Jesus was fulfilling – and those were far more than experiments. As we have looked at the different facets in the preceding chapters, we have come to see that the whole of his mission centred upon the task of redemption, and thus upon the events of the final weeks, especially the cross and resurrection. It was that redemption which Jesus came to achieve and so wonderfully fulfilled, despite what it cost him both in the suffering he endured and the way that he was rejected by his own race and their religious leaders. (Of course we also know that many Jews later became believers in Jesus as their Messiah, and there are many Messianic Jews today.)

At the same time we have seen how Jesus came to proclaim the message of the kingdom of God – the kingdom of heaven – and the way in which Christians down through the centuries, including ourselves in our generation, are to live out membership of that kingdom by our manner of life, both individually and as churches, which we saw as being like colonies of the kingdom.

Christians live and work in the ordinary environment of the world – in many and varied situations in different countries – and are having to live, as it were, like those with a dual membership, both belonging to God's kingdom and living as citizens of their nations. So in their daily lives they are involved in some of the many situations of need around them.

Christians today are finding that as they take the message of the kingdom of God into the world around them, and with it the message of God's love and concern for each and every person, that they find themselves in the midst of, and thus involved in, the heart-breaking situations that surround them. They cannot ignore what is happening, feeling they must put all their efforts into bringing the love of God and the gospel of God to that need, working with him for the alleviation of the particular situation. Others may perhaps read or hear about these concerns and feel that God is calling them to be involved with that as well, whether simply by prayer and concern or through giving, and that may include personal action in self-giving.

So many of these things are indeed very right and proper matters for Christians to be concerned about, matters that we are sure God is deeply concerned about too – we are seeking to carry the gospel, and we need to proclaim the same message as the first apostles. We also show our Christian faith and commitment as we reach out to those in need, those who are suffering, those who are rejected by society around them. It is often only as people see God's love being shown in action that they are willing, even wanting, to hear the Christian message that lies behind it. Jesus was concerned with the people he met, including those who were sick and people who were rejected by society. As his followers, we need to be concerned too.

So today we find that in some places a main Christian effort has been with poverty and social provision for the basic needs of life. It has often been said that it is no use only preaching a gospel of forgiveness and ignoring the 'felt' needs which are predominating in peoples' lives. Jesus himself spoke of this, as recorded in Matthew 6:1–4, 28–34, showing God's concern for the practical needs of life. That message is reinforced with a call in James 2:1–11 to take action. There are many parts of the world where much of the mission of the church is concerned with these things – and through them there can be an opening for the gospel. At times that is expressed in practical help in major disaster situations.

In other areas, Christians are concerned with the needs of those who are being exploited, often for sexual purposes, or caught up with practices that are degrading. There is growing concern over human trafficking. There are those seeking to alleviate and address many injustices. Whatever the need, preaching the gospel does not ignore the situations in which people find themselves.

How right it is for Christians to reach out to those who feel powerless, oppressed, exploited, rejected, or just that they don't count. But as we say this, and we know that Jesus came to proclaim God's love for them from such passages as Luke 4:18–19 (quoting from Isaiah 61:1–2), we nonetheless have to grasp that even these things were going to be secondary in his life to the task of bringing salvation, for it was through this that Jesus was going to bring about the solution to the world's greatest need, the need for forgiveness, righteousness, reconciliation between us and God.

Of course we will want to be involved with the practical outworking of meeting practical needs, with ministry to the oppressed. Sometimes this is through supporting fellow-Christians or Christian agencies who are obeying God's call to action, while at other times there is the joining in with other agencies which are working in these fields. One of the big changes over the past half century or more is in the way that this practical mission has been accepted not just in parts of the church (and this has been a cause of some division between Christians) but by the whole of the world church.

But at the same time, and this has been the main theme in the foregoing chapters, we have to keep firmly in mind the purposes of God revealed to us through the aspects in the life of Jesus that the Lord ordained to be shown to us in the Gospels. Foremost in these we have seen the setting up of God's kingdom in the world, with the churches in different places being like colonies of the kingdom. All that Jesus did led on to redemption through the Cross and resurrection.

As I have been looking at this from the 'chrysalis' standpoint, from seeing the Christian position and message as one who has come towards the end of life here and can no longer be involved with all the activity of Christian ministry, it has enabled me to take a deeply interested but more detached view of the present scene, and to ask whether what is happening (and that includes of course the activities that I have been involved in over sixty years of ministry) is following the priorities that God himself wants us to follow. Have we been – are we – so busy with the nitty-gritty of everyday church life that we have gone off at times at a tangent from God's purposes? Have personal relationships between Christians (or the lack of them) been a hindrance to God's work? Have we been seeking to do what *we* feel to be best, rather than truly waiting upon God to see where he is leading, and what his timing is? Has the desire to have our own perceived needs met, whether personally, as a group or a local congregation, got in the way of God working out his purposes in our own lives?

Probably the greatest need of many Christians today is to give the time that is needed for prayer at the personal level. How can we let God lead and guide us when we come to him for a very hurried few minutes – and yes, I have heard of clergy being so busy that their prayer time has been of that nature – and then all about our 'talking' to him without being open to the messages that he is wanting to bring to us, perhaps by putting thoughts in our minds?

The chrysalis may be looking forward to being a butterfly, with beauty and in an environment that it cannot really understand yet. But this chrysalis is seeking to help those who haven't reached this stage to look carefully at the priorities shown to us, in the four Gospels and elsewhere in Scripture, as being those of God himself.

May God himself bless us with an understanding of his purposes.

APPENDIX

Suggestions for discussion groups, based on each chapter

Introduction

1. Are we so caught up with life here that we are unprepared for what lies ahead?

2. What do we think happens when our life here ends?

3. Do we try to see the Bible's stories and messages from God's perspective?

Chapter 1

1. Are we so set in the mental 'pictures' we have formed and things which we have been taught to believe that we cannot contemplate discovering new truths in the Bible?

2. Can we accept that God only reveals to us that which we need to know?

3. How can we best cope with holding together the truths of Jesus' divinity and humanity?

Chapter 2

1. Why do we need to hold on to the message of the Incarnation?

2. How would you explain to non-Christians the messages in the accounts of the Nativity?

3. What does 'God's publicity plan' say to us about Christian publicity today?

Chapter 3

1. Does the story of the boy Jesus in the Temple have a message about how we treat teenagers?

2. How do we see Jerusalem now, in the twenty-first century, in the light of God's promises and plan?

3. What do we understand about the purposes of God working through the 'silent years'?

Chapter 4

1. Why can't we call John's baptism 'Christian baptism'? What is the difference?

2. Why could the Jews have regular ritual baths, and yet we hold that baptism is a 'once only event'?

3. Is the message of repentance, including turning away and leaving our sins, sufficiently stressed today?

Chapter 5

1. How do we understand 'the kingdom' in today's world?

2. How would you answer a person who says 'I just want to live by following the teaching of the Sermon on the Mount'?

3. Do we see our church in terms of being a colony?

4. What is implied when we speak of Jesus being 'our King'?

Chapter 6

1. Do we ever consider that spirit powers could be at work in people today – even in people around us?

2. Are we alert to Satan exploiting our weak spots?

3. Would you agree that Satan responds to what he sees, rather than having prior knowledge?

Chapter 7

1. What aspect of the Transfiguration account is most helpful to you personally?

2. Do we think enough of the loneliness that can affect Christian leaders, even in a crowded schedule?

3. Are we aware of God's presence with us when we worship and pray, both in church and at home?

Chapter 8

1. Did the thought of the hour dominate all through Jesus' ministry or are we right in seeing his ministry in two sections?

2. Do we see the events during his ministry in terms of him responding to the situation and opportunities, or all as being God-planned?

3. What messages for ourselves do we pick out from the triumphal entry (commemorated on Palm Sunday)?

4. Should we think more about the emotional stress upon Jesus, or is that not our concern?

Chapter 9

1. What does this story have to say to those who feel the Old Testament is irrelevant to them?

2. Do we think enough about the new covenant, and our relationship to God in the light of it?

3. Do we see different acts of commitment in receiving the bread and the wine?

4. Is our attitude in going to Holy Communion more on what we receive or on renewal of love, loyalty and commitment?

Chapter 10

1. What are the most helpful aspects for you within the message of the allegory of the vine?

2. Why do you think Jesus left so much of his teaching about the Holy Spirit to this point?

3. Is the High Priestly prayer more about what has happened or what lies ahead?

4. How much do we heed Jesus' call for unity?

5. The two aspects of Jesus' nature, divine and human, came to the fore in the agony. Do we have parallels to this in our own lives?

Chapter 11

1. Do we place an over-emphasis either on the spiritual message or on the physical suffering of Jesus to the detriment of the other? Can we hold them in a balance that accords with God's purposes?

2. Why did Jesus speak of God forsaking him? Could that have happened or was it just his feelings?

3. Why did Jesus speak of his kingship to Pilate, when he had hardly mentioned it before?

4. How significant to us today is the link between the Passover and the Cross?

Chapter 12

1. How would you describe Jesus' resurrection body?

2. How would you use the resurrection accounts or the different events on that day to help somebody in the 'chrysalis' stage of life?

3. Does it really matter if some find it hard to piece together the various events in the Easter narrative?

4. What would we lack if we were left with the resurrection appearances but did not have the Ascension?

Chapter 13

1. How helpful to you was the analogy of the voyage to the moon?

2. Are there parts of the Christian message, especially in the Gospels, which because some people find them hard to accept, we can treat as non-essential?

3. Is the church today succeeding or failing in seeking to balance the message of the need for salvation, and the task of applying the message of God's love to the issues of justice, poverty and racism?

4. How well are we using our time on earth in the way God wants, and in preparing for life in heaven?